Everyday
People
YOU DON'T MEET
Every Day

Other Works by Scott Gibson

NOVELS

A Year in Stucker's Reach
Stopping By Earth
Welcome to Judelaine
Simon
Standing Outside of Life
Treading Deep Water

PLAYS

(published by Next Stage Press)
Someone Else's Life
Kill the Moment
Six Sour Raspberries
Gallery (a collection of short plays)
Remaining in Orbit

Everyday
People
YOU DON'T MEET
Every Day

*A Collection of Quirky
Short Plays and Monologues*

by

SCOTT GIBSON

PINECONE BOOK COMPANY

ISBN 978-1-949053-01-2

Pinecone Book Company
P.O. Box 65 | Evergreen, Colorado 80437

PineconeBookCo@gmail.com

Dedicated to Alice, Biz and Lorraine

*In memory of all those late nights in the theater
getting another show ready for opening.*

*"My mother writes plays because eight years ago
a typewriter was delivered here by mistake."*

—You Can't Take It With You
George S. Kaufman and Moss Hart

Contents

Playwright's Preface

Greetings, fellow theater lovers!

The short plays and monologues contained behind this preface are the product of what I think of as my *Golden Retriever brain*. Just as that particular breed of canine has a predilection for picking up things it finds along the way (sticks, bones, etc.), my mind seems similarly wired to go out and find random items—often without my permission or even my knowledge—and bring them back for contemplation.

That's the best explanation I can offer for the majority of the pieces found in this book. Most began as scraps of ideas and scenarios that were simply *there* one day. Apparently it was up to me to take what my wayward brain laid at my feet and flesh it into something resembling a dramatic masterpiece. You, the reader, can be the judge of where, when and whether I succeeded.

Some of these plays have been produced at various theaters around the country. A few have won awards. Others are presented here for the very first time.

To actors seeking potential monologues to use as audition pieces, I offer any of the pieces in this book to you without restriction or cost. If you see something you think might showcase your abilities to their best effect, feel free to use it. And good luck!

To theater teachers looking for material that might in some way be useful in helping your students hone their craft, I extend the same courtesy.

To theater companies and/or artistic directors seeking to put together an evening of short plays, if you should find something here that you feel might work well on your stage, let's talk! Like any playwright, I'm thrilled anytime someone has an interest in staging one of my pieces. E-mail me at **ScottConundrum@hotmail.com** and let's see if we can work out some sort of mutually satisfactory arrangement.

In the meantime, turn the page and see if you can't find a compelling scenario or a quirky character or two among the plays that follow.

Act One
PLAYS

Scrapbooking for Fun and Relaxation

CHARACTERS

VICTORIA and AUSTIN, a married couple

SET REQUIREMENTS

A table and two chairs on an otherwise empty stage

VICTORIA sits at a table working at scrapbooking. AUSTIN enters. He wears a shirt and pants that have several smudges and a few minor tears.

VICTORIA. Hey, Bear.
AUSTIN. Hey, Pooh.

AUSTIN flops down in a chair on the opposite side of the table.

VICTORIA. You were making quite a racket for a while. What were you doing up there?
AUSTIN. Nothing much.

AUSTIN picks up some of VICTORIA's scrapbooking items and turns them over idly in his hands.

AUSTIN. Just moving some stuff. Trying out a few ideas.
VICTORIA. Oh?
AUSTIN. Yeah… By the way… That little antique table back in the at-

tic alcove…

VICTORIA. Mm-hm?

AUSTIN. How attached were you to that?

VICTORIA. Well, it was my grandmother's. But it's not in very good shape. That's why it's up there. Why? Did something happen?

AUSTIN. Not really… It tipped over, is all.

VICTORIA. You bumped into it?

AUSTIN. Sort of.

VICTORIA. Did one of the legs break off, or something? When it fell?

AUSTIN. I don't know yet. I haven't been out to look.

VICTORIA stops working on her scrapbook and looks at him.

VICTORIA. "Out?"

AUSTIN. It went out the window.

VICTORIA. The attic window?

AUSTIN nods.

VICTORIA. I didn't even know that window opened.

AUSTIN. It doesn't. Well, it didn't used to.

VICTORIA. Then, how… ?

AUSTIN. Do you know how a fulcrum works?

VICTORIA. That's a kind of a lever, isn't it?

AUSTIN. *(nodding)* Looks a little bit like a teeter-totter. It allows a person to stand on one end and lift things much heavier than they are.

VICTORIA. You had a fulcrum up there?

AUSTIN. I made one, yes. With a couple of boxes and a plank of wood.

VICTORIA. And… what were you attempting to lift?

AUSTIN. You know that old couch?

VICTORIA. You were trying to move the couch? All by yourself?

AUSTIN. Just a little ways. From the middle of the room to over by the wall.

VICTORIA. That's an awfully big couch, Bear. To be moving by yourself.

AUSTIN. Yeah… Well, it's not as heavy as it looks. It's surprisingly light, in fact. I probably didn't need the fulcrum at all. I definitely didn't need to jump off the credenza onto the other end of the board.

VICTORIA. Oh… really?

AUSTIN. It was sort of amazing, really. How high that couch went.

VICTORIA. High…?

AUSTIN. I wish I'd gotten it on video. That's the kind of thing that would get a million hits on YouTube.

VICTORIA. The couch?

AUSTIN. Oh… Did it belong to your grandmother, as well?

VICTORIA. No… Did the couch land on the little table?

AUSTIN. Oh, no, it didn't go anywhere near the table. I'm not sure where it went, in fact.

VICTORIA. You don't know?

AUSTIN. I kept thinking it would come back down through the hole it made, but it never did.

VICTORIA. The hole?

AUSTIN. *(nodding)* In the roof.

VICTORIA. There's a hole in the roof, now?

AUSTIN. It was the squirrels, I think. They were what knocked over the table.

VICTORIA. Squirrels?

AUSTIN. When the couch went through the roof, a whole bunch of stuff fell in through the hole. Including a big old squirrels' nest. And the squirrels that were in it.

VICTORIA. There are squirrels in the attic, now?

AUSTIN. Well, not just now. I mean, technically, they were there before. They're just a little bit more in the attic than they used to be. *(glancing upward)* And maybe also upstairs. One or two of them might have fallen through the hole in the bedroom ceiling.

VICTORIA. There's… there's also a hole in the ceiling?

AUSTIN. I was chasing them with a broom. I suppose it may have been the broom that knocked over the table. But then the squirrels started ganging up on me. They apparently have a pack mentality. Do you think that there might be squirrel gangs running around the neighborhood? Terrorizing dogs and cats, and warring with other squirrel gangs?

VICTORIA. Could you get back to the hole in the bedroom ceiling?

AUSTIN. Oh, yeah… So the squirrels chased me up on top of that old cedar chest. You know the one I'm talking about.

VICTORIA. *(nodding)* Yes.

AUSTIN. So, I'm trying to fend them off with the broom, and all of a sudden, I hear this weird cracking noise. The squirrels and I stop moving, and we all look at each other with a kind of a knowing glance… like when you sense that something's about to happen, but you aren't quite sure what it's going to be? So, we're frozen like that for ten seconds or so, and then I guess most of them figured out what was about to happen, so they lit out of there like crazy, just before the floorboards kind of… I don't know… disintegrated, I guess you'd say? The next thing I know, the cedar chest and I have bounced off the bed, and the chest went one direction, and I went a different one. *(thinks about this for a second)* Boy, it was a lucky thing the bed was right below where I fell through the ceiling, wasn't it?

AUSTIN picks up another item from the scrapbooking materials and examines it.

AUSTIN. This looks nice. So, where are you going to put it?

VICTORIA. So, you're telling me our bedroom is pretty much destroyed now?

AUSTIN. Well, not the whole thing. *(beat)* Just the bed part.

VICTORIA stares at AUSTIN for a few seconds, sighs, and lowers her head.

AUSTIN. Oh, and Pooh?

VICTORIA. Yes, Bear?

AUSTIN. When you reach a stopping point… When it's convenient for you…

VICTORIA. Uh-huh?

AUSTIN lifts his shirt just slightly to display an ugly-looking series of red marks on his side.

AUSTIN. I'm thinking I should have somebody take a look at this squirrel-bite.

VICTORIA. *(sighs)* Sure. I'll get my car keys.

VICTORIA stands and crosses a few steps.

AUSTIN. On the bright side, this gives you something more to put in your scrapbook. If you were running out of ideas.

VICTORIA. Yes, Bear. Now I have a lot more ideas.

VICTORIA exits. AUSTIN rubs the back of his head. He has a thoughtful expression.

AUSTIN. *(calling to VICTORIA)* Do you think we could train a squirrel to be a house pet? *(rubbing his head)* Maybe that's just the concussion talking…

The lights fade as he continues to rub the back of his head and ponders this.

END OF PLAY

Then Paupers Would Ride

("Then Paupers Would Ride" had its world premiere in May 2016 at Carrollwood Players in Tampa, Florida.)

CHARACTERS
KEITH and ANNA, both in their mid to late 20s

SET REQUIREMENTS
Two stools on an otherwise empty stage

Lights up on a stage occupied only by two tall stools, one stage left and one stage right.

KEITH sits on the stage left stool. ANNA sits on the stage right stool. Both wear dark shirts and slacks; ANNA has an unknotted red scarf around her neck, both ends trailing down in front of her.

A few seconds pass before the dialogue begins.

KEITH. I met her at church camp when we were both seventeen. Well, no; that's not exactly true. I had known who she was for years. We'd gone all the way through school together, though I can't remember ever exchanging a single word in all that time. Our families went to the same church, so I saw her there, as well. Things are *(searches for the word)* more casual there. Friendlier. If we happened to look in each other's direction at the same time, we'd smile. It didn't mean anything, of course. Just a kind of acknowledgment.

ANNA. I signed up to be a counselor the summer between high school and college. Everyone in my family is kind of outdoorsy. We've hiked and canoed and fished for as long as I can remember, and I have younger siblings, so it seemed like a pretty good fit. It was a lot of fun, actually… sing-alongs and roasting hot dogs and marshmallows and swimming. Mixed in with the occasional scraped knee and bee sting. And little kids puking up hot dogs and marshmallows when they'd had too many.

KEITH. If you'd gone to high school with me, you'd… Well, you probably wouldn't have remembered me. I'm one of those people who just sort of blended in. Not a star athlete, not super smart, but I did okay. I didn't run with the popular crowd, but I had friends. I wasn't a weirdo, if you know what I mean. But *she*—

ANNA. It put me in a different world, though. I don't mean I felt out of place or anything. It's just that none of my friends—well, what you'd call my *regular friends*—went to my church, so I didn't really know any of the staff or the other junior counselors too well.

KEITH. —she was definitely one of the A-listers. A cheerleader. Homecoming Queen. That kind of stuff. Popular with everybody. Just, well, in most circumstances, out of my league. Except for that summer.

ANNA. He was what you'd call a sweet guy. Boy Scout-type. I remembered him from Sunday school classes and around school. Just always kind of hovering in the background. *(laughs)* I guess that makes me sound kind of shallow, and it isn't that… I hope. It's just that we seemed to move in different orbits.

KEITH. I'd been a counselor for three years, so maybe I just felt more comfortable, more in my element. Plus, well, we were sort of thrust together a lot of the time. On hikes, and helping the kids with crafts. And campfire activities—songs and ghost stories. It's funny how, when you don't feel the pressure to be—I don't know… *cool?*—when you don't feel like you have to be somebody you're not, you can just relax.

ANNA. It was just a few days into camp when one of the kids tripped over a tree root or something, and she was lying on the ground holding her leg and screaming. She wouldn't let me look at it, and I was in a panic that she'd broken something. He happened to come along, and I don't know what it was... he just knew how to handle the situation, I guess. He was calm and efficient and just talked to her real quietly, and she took away her hands and let him look at the scrape. He was so matter-of-fact about it all, and you could tell she totally trusted him. I was so relieved to have him handle things. It's probably the first time I ever really stopped and looked at him.

KEITH. Maybe it was because we both just *clicked* with the kids—she was sweet and pretty, and I could make them laugh—the counselors just sort of put us together on projects. Like the talent show. There's nothing like wrangling two dozen seven- to ten-year-olds to force you to bond with somebody.

ANNA. I know it's not nice to say, but we would sometimes get to laughing so hard over those kids. Watching some of them try to learn a dance, or listening to them sing off-key. Or trying to get them to memorize a simple sentence or two. We started calling the place "Camp Notta Lotta Talent." Only to each other, of course.

KEITH. It was fun getting to know someone up close after watching her from afar for so long. *(beat)* You know, that sounds creepier than I meant it to. It wasn't as though I was stalking her. At least, not then.

ANNA. He wasn't somebody I probably would ever have gotten to know very well, if I hadn't decided to volunteer at camp that summer. *(beat)* It makes me realize that the world is probably full of people we are around a lot, and yet we never really get to know. We never get to see how kind, or funny, or capable they may be, because we just don't take the time.

KEITH. I wish sometimes we'd never had that summer together. I wish I'd just continued to look at her from a distance.

ANNA. We kind of started... seeking each other out, you know? After the kids were in their bunks, or just in the mess hall, we'd wind up sitting at the same table. It wasn't anything romantic, we were just buds, you know?

KEITH. It's an amazing feeling, to actually have the popular girl walk into a room and look around, and you know she's looking for *you*.

ANNA. He'd make me laugh. And the way he could handle those kids, keep them in line without even trying. That impressed me.

KEITH. But it's such an artificial atmosphere… summer camp. I started to forget that. I started to think there was something more there.

ANNA. I guess, maybe, I was lying to myself a little bit. And, by default, to him. There was a little romantic element to what was going on, I know. Now, don't get me wrong… I never was *that* kind of a girl. I don't lead guys on; I don't mess around casually. We'd kind of bump shoulders now and then. Lean against each other by the campfire. Catch each other's glance from across a room with those "Can you believe *that* just happened?" kind of moments.

KEITH. If that summer could have just gone on a little longer. *(rueful laugh)* Like, maybe another five years or so… Then it might actually have turned into something. Instead, well…

ANNA. Turns out, we were going to the same community college that fall.

KEITH. We were both still living at home, and I talked her into being a youth group leader at our church. It seemed like a way to keep the connection we'd made that summer going.

ANNA. But so were a lot of my other friends from high school. I mean, these were the people I'd hung around with for years. I… I don't know.

KEITH. That wasn't such a great idea. You never really want to coax somebody into doing something they aren't real interested in doing. They aren't happy. And then you aren't happy, either, because you can tell they don't really want to be there.

ANNA. I'd like to say I made kind of an effort to bring him into my group of friends. But, well, it wasn't a good fit. All that happened was I realized that when we weren't surrounded by a bunch of eight-year-old kids in the woods, we really didn't have a lot to talk about.

KEITH. I should have just let it go… let *her* go. She started finding reasons for missing the youth group meetings.

ANNA. I met a guy in one of my classes. We just clicked, you know? We started studying together, but that was just an excuse, really.

KEITH. One night, she called and said she couldn't make it; she had extra assignments to do. I… I did a stupid thing.

ANNA. We could both tell this could lead to something more. And it did.

KEITH. I started following her. I knew her class schedule, and her routine. I mean, even then, I knew I was crossing some sort of a line, but… I don't know. There was a kind of desperation, I guess. I just wanted that feeling we'd had all summer long back again.

ANNA. *(glancing over at KEITH)* Those weeks at camp felt more and more like a dream, something that had happened to somebody else, not to me. I was back in my real life again. I dropped the church activities altogether. I told him I was just too busy, and he seemed to understand. That was that, I thought. I barely even saw him on campus any more.

KEITH. It was like I was standing outside my own body, watching what I was doing, knowing how crazy it was, but I couldn't stop myself. I'd check every day to see if she was going to class. I'd swing by the library every night to watch her. And… that other guy. If they weren't there, then I'd sit outside her house, waiting until she got there. And it was nearly always with him.

ANNA. One night in the library, I happened to look up and catch a glimpse of him in a mirror. These big, curved mirrors they have at the front of the aisles, I guess so that the librarians can check and make sure people aren't back in the stacks making out or something. So he didn't see me see *him.* He was just leaning out from one of the shelves, watching… And I got the strangest feeling. It was the look on his face, I guess. Something I'd never seen before, and it made me feel… *(shudders)* I told myself he just happened to be there, and that he probably wasn't even looking at me at all. But I didn't really believe it.

KEITH. It was seeing that other guy, I guess. This guy she hadn't even known as long as she'd known me, and now, he was acting like she belonged to him. And she seemed *okay* with that.

ANNA. After that, maybe my awareness was heightened. I realized I was seeing him other places, too. Places that he didn't... Well, I guess I shouldn't say that he didn't *belong,* because it's a free country. But still, I knew he wasn't just *there.* He was there because I was.

KEITH. Whatever we had, whatever we'd shared, it was gone. If I didn't know that already, I knew it for sure when she came up to me one day. For once, I hadn't been following her. I was cleaning up after the youth group meeting, emptying the trash, and I was coming back into the building from the dumpster, and there she was. It was dark, and it really caught me off guard. I wasn't expecting to see anybody.

Now ANNA and KEITH turn on their stools to face each other.

ANNA. "How does it feel?"

KEITH. "What? How does *what* feel?"

ANNA. "To have someone following you around? Spying on you?"

KEITH. "What are you talking about?"

ANNA. "I've seen you. A bunch of times now. In the library. At the Cineplex one time. You were parked across the street from my house one night."

KEITH. "No..."

ANNA. "Don't lie. I know your car. I know what I've seen."

KEITH. "I mean, I wasn't spying on you. I was... I was just concerned..."

Both ANNA and KEITH face forward again.

KEITH. The more I tried to make her understand, the worse I made everything. All I wanted, I think, was for her to know that I was just a regular guy, not some crazy, not some sicko.

ANNA. I wasn't angry. Irritated, was all. Puzzled. He said, "I miss what we had."

KEITH. She said, "What do you mean, what we had?"

ANNA. He said, "You know… that… that friendship from last summer."

KEITH. "Well… well, that's still there," she said.

ANNA. *(shaking her head)* He said it wasn't the same. He asked about Bret.

KEITH. "Who's that guy, anyway?"

ANNA. "He's someone from my economics class. A friend."

KEITH. "He's more than a friend, isn't he?"

ANNA stands and crosses down front.

ANNA. I mean, I had to have known. I had to have known it was jealousy. But all summer long, he'd been so down-to-earth. He was so good with those kids, you know?

KEITH. I just… in those few seconds… I watched it all fall apart. I just wanted to make her see that I was *normal.*

ANNA. I shouldn't have gone there that night, not alone. But it seemed like the forthright thing to do. I wasn't scared. I don't think I was scared, not up until…

KEITH stands and crosses down front. Both he and ANNA address the audience directly.

KEITH. Even then, she was nice, she was trying to be nice. Trying to explain, trying so hard. And I could feel the distance between us get wider and wider, as she explained that she'd never had "those kinds of feelings" about me. That we were friends, and that she was sorry if I'd misinterpreted things, or if she'd accidentally led me on in any way…

ANNA. It was October. A chilly night. He was just in his shirtsleeves, since he was only outside long enough to empty the trash. I could see my breath, and his. He was shivering.

KEITH. It was dark, and cold, and quiet.

ANNA. I told him I hoped he understood. That I'd never intended to hurt him or…

KEITH turns to face ANNA.

KEITH. She smiled at me, and turned away. I didn't want her to go; I couldn't let it end that way.

ANNA. He startled me when he put his hands on my shoulders. His grip was so tight.

ANNA turns to face KEITH.

KEITH. "I just want to make you understand."

ANNA. "Let go. You're scaring me."

KEITH. She yelled. Screamed, actually.

ANNA. "Let go! Let *go* of me!"

KEITH. I just… I wanted her to be quiet! I never meant… I was never going to…

ANNA takes hold of the ends of her scarf, looking at KEITH.

KEITH's hands dangle at his sides. His fingers twitch.

ANNA. I realized what an awful, awful mistake I'd made.

KEITH. "Please! Please, listen! I'm not going to hurt you!"

KEITH faces forward.

KEITH. …But…But… I did. *(fighting back emotion)* I just wanted her to stop screaming…

ANNA. The sky overhead. The black sky… Was the last thing I saw.

ANNA faces forward.

KEITH. I have no right to be sorry… But I am.

ANNA. I know.

KEITH. I used to think, "That's not who I am. I am not that person! I am not a person who does something like that." *(beat)* It was only later that I came to realize that I had it all backwards. I was never *not* that person. I just didn't know it until that night.

ANNA takes hold of one end of the scarf, pulling on it until the opposite end slides around her neck and drops to the floor at her feet.

ANNA. I thought there would be more to my life. I never dreamt…

KEITH. In the alley behind my church. Of all places, it was in the alley behind my church!!! God will never forgive me.

ANNA turns to face KEITH. She crosses to stand close to him.

ANNA. I do.

KEITH. Don't. Please, don't…

ANNA puts her arms around him, pulling his head to rest on her shoulder.

ANNA. You don't have a choice.

KEITH. Please.

ANNA. Shh. Shh.

KEITH. *(whispering)* No…

The lights fade.

END OF PLAY

Taking Away the Sting

CHARACTERS
MARK, KENT and AMY
Any ages; all are riding on a city bus

SET REQUIREMENTS
Six chairs

Lights up on six chairs situated on an otherwise empty stage. Two chairs sit side by side, slightly right of center. These represent two seats on a city bus. Two more chairs sit a few feet behind and slightly left of center. These represent another row of seats on the bus, on the opposite side of the aisle. Still another pair of chairs sits even further upstage, center, representing the very last row of seats on the bus.

At rise, KENT, a man in business attire, sits on the stage-right chair in the front row. A briefcase or bag sits by his feet, and he is listening to music through earbuds. AMY, also in business attire, occupies one of the seats on the stage-left side. She reads from a book or iPad.

A moment passes, and MARK, in business attire and carrying a shoulder bag, enters right as if he has just boarded the bus. He sits in the seat next to KENT. MARK smiles at KENT, who glances at him, smiles and nods in response.

MARK. Good morning.
KENT. Hey.

MARK gets himself situated, settling into his chair and placing the bag by his feet. He turns in his seat to look back at AMY, and waves. She smiles at him.

AMY. Hi.

MARK turns around again. He bends down and unzips his bag. After a few seconds, he pulls out a small gift-wrapped item. He sits up straight and, smiling, hands it to KENT. KENT pulls the ear buds out of his ears and looks down at the package.

KENT. What's this?
MARK. Open it.
KENT. What's… what's it for?
MARK. Go ahead.

With some misgivings, KENT unwraps the package as MARK, beaming, looks on. KENT holds up a small potted plant.

KENT. It's a plant.
MARK. Uh-huh. An aloe! If you get a sunburn or a cut or something, you can break off a little piece and rub it on the injury. It helps it heal, and takes away the sting.

KENT, speechless, stares at the potted plant in his hands.

MARK. Just give it a little water—not too much—maybe once a week, and it'll be fine. I recommend setting it on the windowsill over your kitchen sink. That'll remind you. It'll do well with some sun. And it will get a lot bigger. Eventually, you'll want to transplant it into a bigger container. You can even divide it and start separate plants.

KENT. I'm sorry… I guess I don't understand. This… This is for me?

MARK nods.

KENT. Why?
MARK. It's a gift.
KENT. Well, I got that part. I just don't know why.
MARK. It's a celebration. We have been riding the bus together for a year, now. A year today!

KENT looks dubiously down at the plant and then even more dubiously at MARK.

KENT. We have? You've... You've actually been keeping track?
MARK. I thought a little memento was in order. *(beat)* Oh, and don't worry. I don't expect anything in return. I just wanted to mark the occasion. Ha! That's funny!
KENT. It is?
MARK. Well, yeah. I accidentally made a pun. Because I said "mark the occasion," and my name's Mark.
KENT. I... I don't know what to say.
MARK. You don't have to say anything at all.
KENT. This just seems sort of weird.
MARK. Weird? Why weird?
KENT. Well... because we don't really know each other. I mean, I know who you are, because I see you on the bus a lot. *(holding up the potted plant)* For an entire year now, apparently. But I don't *know* you. Until just now, I didn't even know your name was Mark. And you don't know mine.
MARK. It's Kent.
KENT. *(taken aback)* How do you know that?
MARK. We've been commuting together for the past fifty-two weeks.
KENT. That doesn't explain—
MARK. Do you have any idea how many times I've been sitting here—or nearby—when you take out your phone? You always answer it, "This

is Kent."

KENT. Oh.

MARK. So, you see, it's not weird.

KENT looks at the plant and then tries to hand it back to MARK.

KENT. Look, I... I appreciate the gesture, but I'm not really a plant guy. I wouldn't know what to do with this.

MARK. I just told you what to do. Set it in your window and give it a little water. It doesn't require much attention. It isn't really a commitment.

KENT. *(shaking his head)* No. No, you should keep this.

MARK. *(refusing to take it back)* I don't need it. I have lots of them already. This one is for you.

KENT. I don't want it!

KENT thrusts the plant at MARK, who reluctantly takes it back. MARK stares down at the plant. A few seconds pass.

KENT. Look... This is uncomfortable for me. We're not friends. We're not acquaintances. We're just two people who happen to ride the same bus to work sometimes.

MARK. For a whole year, now.

KENT. Yeah, well... whatever. This just isn't... well, it isn't normal. People who don't know each other very well don't exchange gifts. It's strange. It's awkward.

MARK continues to look down at the plant. A few seconds pass. KENT glances at him.

KENT. *(gesturing)* Look at everybody. There are buses all over the city, all over the country, filled with people on their way someplace. Nobody... *Nobody* on any of them is giving anybody else a gift. Everybody is just riding, minding their own business, on their way to their own lives, their jobs, their errands. You understand that, don't you?… Don't you?

MARK. *(nodding)* Sure.

MARK takes the wrapping paper from around the plant, folds it as neatly as he can manage, then tucks it into his bag. He picks up his bag and stands. He crosses up the "aisle" and goes to sit in one of the seats toward the back. As he passes AMY, she smiles at him, but he does not seem to notice.

Once seated, he puts his bag on the floor and sets the potted plant on the seat beside him. He averts his head, appearing to gaze out a side window.

KENT sighs, then puts his earbuds back into his ears. AMY glances over her shoulder back at MARK, who does not return her glance. She waits a second or two, debating, then stands and crosses down to sit next to KENT. KENT glances at her.

AMY. Could we talk for a moment?

KENT. *(lifting his earbud away from his ear)* What?

AMY. You aren't the only one.

KENT. Excuse me?

AMY. The plant… You're not the only person he's given one of those to.

KENT. You're kidding me.

AMY. He gave me one last year.

KENT. What did you do?

AMY. I took it, of course.

KENT. You did?

AMY. It was a gift.

KENT. Do you know that guy?

AMY. Not very well. About as much as you do, I suppose.

KENT. Didn't you think that was odd?

AMY. Yes. As a matter of fact, I did.

KENT. Then why did you accept it?

AMY. Because he wanted me to have it. And what does it hurt, after all, to take something that it clearly gave him pleasure to offer?

KENT. Because you don't know where something like that might lead.

AMY glances over her shoulder in MARK's direction, then faces forward again.

AMY. Meaning?

KENT. You might be sending him the wrong message. You might… You might be leading him on.

AMY. Ah! And he might start stalking me, or something.

KENT. Well… yes.

AMY. After one full year of riding on the same bus…

KENT. Maybe. Who knows how these people's minds work?

AMY. "These people." So, now, he's one of "these people"? Because he wanted to give you a stupid plant.

KENT. *(sighing heavily)* Look… All I want to do is just go to work. To sit here, minding my own business, not bothering anybody, and not having anybody bother me. That's what most people want to do, right? They're not riding the bus to make new friends; they just want to go someplace, that's all.

AMY. Oh. *(starting to get up)* Sorry.

KENT. And now, it's all awkward. All because somebody keeps track of how many days I've been commuting on the same bus as him. What am I supposed to do now? Start taking an earlier bus? Or drive?

AMY. *(sitting back down next to him again)* It might have been a lot less awkward if you'd just taken his gift and said thank you. You're the one who's turned this into a much bigger deal than it needed to be. I mean, look at me: not that much has changed. Mark says hello to me each day, and I say hello back. And I have an aloe plant at home that has grown to gigantic proportions. Life isn't really all that different than before.

KENT. *(another sigh)* And this started out as such an uncomplicated day.

AMY. Yeah, well.

AMY gets up and crosses back to sit in her original seat.

KENT puts his earbuds back into his ears. After only a few seconds, he removes them again. He thinks for another few seconds, then stands, and crosses up the "aisle." He looks at AMY as he passes her. She doesn't look at him, but smiles as he passes. KENT crosses up and picks up the plant that is sitting on the empty seat. He sits down, holding the plant in his lap.

KENT. A whole year, huh?

MARK doesn't say anything.

KENT. Where does the time go?

MARK doesn't say anything.

KENT. Look… I'm sorry. I realize I was being really ungracious before. It just… you just caught me by surprise. Nobody's ever given me a gift on the bus before.

MARK. And I doubt anybody ever will again.

KENT. *(trying not to smile)* No. Probably not. Anyway, I just want to apologize.

MARK nods.

KENT. And… and if the offer still stands…

KENT holds up the plant and looks at MARK.

MARK. I don't think it would be happy at your place.

MARK looks away. KENT considers this for a second. Finally he stands and puts the potted plant back on the empty chair.

KENT. Probably not. But thank you. For thinking of me on our... our anniversary of... of bus-riding.

KENT crosses back down and takes his original seat again. AMY is busy reading her book/iPad.

A moment passes. MARK faces forward. Then, as if arriving at a decision, he picks up the plant, crosses down the "aisle" and places the plant on the empty seat next to KENT. He turns and crosses back up a few steps, then pauses and talks over his shoulder in KENT's direction.

MARK. Remember: Not too much water. Just a little bit.

MARK crosses back up and sits in the back row of seats. KENT looks down at the potted plant, then puts his earbuds on again. AMY, still reading, smiles.

The lights fade.

END OF PLAY

He's With Me

CHARACTERS

LANCE, business executive, late 20s/early 30s
REBECCA, ORRIN, CARLA, also business executives, any age
PONY, a 10-year-old boy, a figment of LANCE's imagination

SET REQUIREMENTS

A long table to serve as a conference table,
four chairs surrounding the table

Lights up on a conference table surrounded by several chairs. A few office personnel in business attire are seated around the table: LANCE, REBECCA, ORRIN and CARLA. At rise, they are in the midst of a meeting. Various folders are strewn across the table.

REBECCA. I think we can all agree that we have to set aside the Magruder proposal. It's just not feasible. We good with that?

General nodding and sounds of assent. REBECCA sets aside a folder.

REBECCA. What do we think about Gates and French?
ORRIN. Well, the price is in our ballpark.
CARLA. I think we're focusing too much on the financial side of things. I can appreciate keeping an eye on the bottom line, but not at the expense of targeting the right changes.
ORRIN. Spoken like a marketing person.
CARLA. *(grinning)* Take off your accounting visor for a minute, Orrin,

and think outside the box.

REBECCA. I'm a little concerned about where we fall on their list of priorities. I get the feeling they'd assign us to their 'B' team.

PONY enters. He's dressed like 10-year-old boy wearing jeans and a t-shirt smudged with dirt and some colorful stain (Kool-Aid, candy or something). His hair is unkempt, and he grins broadly. He leaps, rather than walks, into the room.

Nobody notices his arrival. The meeting continues uninterrupted. PONY makes a broad, wacky face at LANCE, who notices, but makes no reaction. Throughout most of PONY's subsequent antics, LANCE shows no reaction, unless noted. Nobody else ever reacts at all.

CARLA. I'm inclined to think that their 'B' people are better than the first-string team at Zander Concepts.

PONY runs around the table two or three times.

ORRIN. Look at you: A sports analogy and everything.

REBECCA. Is Taylor still working at Gates? He'd be a good person to have on the account. If we could get him.

CARLA. I think he's still there. I'll check.

ORRIN. Yeah, but will Gates and French give us something more than off-the-shelf templates? I'd like to have something unique. Customized.

PONY stands behind ORRIN, jumping up and down.

PONY. *(chanting)* Unique! Customized! Wow, wow, wow!

REBECCA. That's a point. If we're going to put the time and resources into this kind of a paradigm shift, then we go for something bold and defined. Not something that looks just a little bit different than what anybody else is doing.

PONY moves to stand next to Rebecca's chair. He holds a hand over her coffee mug, forefinger extended downward, as though he is about to plunge it into her coffee. He continues to fake doing this, clearly trying to draw LANCE's attention. He covers his mouth with his other hand and giggles as he does this.

PONY. Whoops! Here it goes! Whoops! Oh, nooooooo!

ORRIN. I honestly think the Zander proposal is more in line with what we want.

REBECCA. Well, we aren't tied to any one of these three, as far as that goes.

PONY. As far as that goes.

REBECCA. We're flexible. We can go out looking some more.

PONY. We're flexible. We can go out looking some more.

REBECCA. There's no point in rushing things. We're paying these people, after all.

Now PONY stands slightly behind REBECCA, mimicking her facial expressions as she talks.

REBECCA. They can cool their heels until we know which way we want to go. I think we all have plenty of experience in moving too hastily and then regretting it afterward. There's no set timeline for making the shift, so let's do this right.

PONY's ongoing mimicking is getting to be too much for LANCE. He begins to crack a smile.

REBECCA. Lance? You're awfully quiet. You have any thoughts on this?

LANCE, startled, clears his throat and leans forward in his chair, sobering.

LANCE. I do think we should take Magruder out of the running.

PONY. Magruder! *(trying the word several different ways)* Mah-GROO-der! Mah-GROODY GROOD GROODER!

LANCE. Zander is definitely cutting edge, but—

PONY. But! But, but but!!! My finger smells like butt!

LANCE *can't help but chuckle at this. The other adults look at him oddly.*

LANCE. *(trying to cover his laugh with a cough)* Sorry. Something caught in my throat… *(clearing his throat)* Has anybody seen what Zander did for the Marshfield Group? The direction they're taking them?

ORRIN. Oh, who cares? That's a whole other arena. No overlap at all.

REBECCA. No, Lance makes a good point. Maybe we want to check with somebody over there and see how Zander's program is working for them.

PONY *has now gotten down on all fours and is crawling under the table.*

CARLA. I'm hearing they're not real happy…

PONY. Underpants, underpants, I can see your underpants!

REBECCA. Well, let's not go with hearsay. You know what? I can make a call. I'm pretty tight with Walter. He'll talk off the record.

ORRIN. Hey, what about Boister? I know they're a start-up, without much of a track record, but they've got to be hungry. They'd work hard for us.

REBECCA. *(nodding)* Put them on the list. And Carla, did you ever hear anything back from Pearl?

CARLA. Yeah, didn't you get my email? They won't talk to us for anything under twenty K.

REBECCA. Oh, yeah, I did see that. I forgot. Sorry. Well, screw 'em.

PONY emerges from the other side of the table. He gets to his feet.

PONY. Screw 'em! Screw 'em, blue 'em, then tattoo 'em!

He runs around the conference table with his arms extended like an airplane. He makes motor noises with his mouth.

REBECCA. *(glancing at her phone)* Well, it's quarter 'til. I've got a conference call in fifteen.

PONY stops abruptly.

PONY. Hey! Who farted?

PONY sniffs the air suspiciously.

CARLA. Well, I'll check in with Taylor. See if maybe they're doing custom stuff now.
PONY. It smells really bad...
ORRIN. I'll talk to somebody at Boister. Have them work up a proposal for us.

REBECCA stands.

REBECCA. You know, while you're at it, touch base with Terrill and Soames, too. Just to cover our bases.
PONY. *(pointing at REBECCA)* It was her! She tooted! She tooted, and it smells like cabbage!

LANCE is fighting a losing battle, trying hard not to laugh or at least snicker.

ORRIN. You okay?

LANCE. *(choking back tears)* I don't know what it is… An allergy maybe.

CARLA. *(standing)* I've got some antihistamines in my desk.

LANCE. *(with difficulty)* Thanks. I'll be okay.

ORRIN stands. He and CARLA exchange a puzzled glance. PONY stands to one side, jumping up and down and spinning around.

REBECCA. Okay, let's talk tomorrow. How's eight for everybody?

ORRIN. Works for me.

CARLA. Me, too.

LANCE. I can do that.

REBECCA exits. ORRIN and CARLA follow her out, talking.

CARLA. What are you doing for lunch?

ORRIN. I'm eating at my desk.

CARLA. You kidding me? Again?

They exit.

LANCE exhales a sigh of relief. PONY stops jumping. He sags with exhaustion, and crosses to sink into a chair some distance away from LANCE. He studies LANCE solemnly.

LANCE. Oh, man. Oh, brother. That was too close.

PONY. *(admonishing)* When are you going to grow up, Lance?

LANCE. Sorry.

PONY. This is just ridiculous. What am I doing here?

LANCE. *(wiping his eyes)* I don't know…

PONY. The hell you don't. You get bored, your mind drifts…

LANCE. Well, can you blame me?

PONY. Yes, I can, as a matter of fact. *(gesturing)* Look around you. This is a place of business.

LANCE. (*nodding*) I know…

PONY. Do you? *Do you?* I'm not real sure about that. "Underpants?" "Tooting?" You're not ten years old anymore.

Beat. PONY looks at LANCE, who does not look up at PONY.

PONY. You've got to let me go. Now. Today.

LANCE. Yeah.

PONY. This was fun when we were both kids. But one of us has got to grow up…

PONY reaches across the table to put his hand atop LANCE's.

PONY. And it can't be me. I wasn't made for that.

LANCE. I know.

PONY. You understand?

LANCE. (*nodding*) I do.

PONY. I belong to some other little kid, now. It's time to let go.

Beat.

LANCE heaves a very large sigh. He looks up at PONY. They smile at each other. PONY stands and extends his hand to LANCE. LANCE shakes it.

PONY. Still friends?

LANCE. Friends forever.

PONY. All right, then.

PONY walks across the room and exits.

LANCE remains seated for a few seconds. Finally, he stands and begins to stack up all the items left on the table. He has nearly com-

pleted this when PONY re-enters one last time. LANCE does not see him at first.

PONY. Hey.

LANCE turns and looks at him.

PONY. One last one for the road…

PONY takes a deep breath and runs around the table one final time.

PONY. *(yelling as he runs)* Farty fart fart fart! Farty fart fart fart!

He finishes up by turning in front of LANCE and sticking his rear out at him. He makes a final, extended fart noise by sticking out his tongue and blowing through his lips. Lance grins throughout this.

Then PONY turns to LANCE.

PONY. Are we good?

LANCE. *(laughs)* We're good.

PONY exits running, waving his arms over his head and yelling exuberantly. His yelling gets fainter as he runs down the hallway. Finally, it can no longer be heard at all. LANCE stands listening until all is quiet again.

Smiling, he picks up the stack of items from the table and exits, shutting off the light.

END OF PLAY

Meanwhile, in the Back Seat

*("Meanwhile, in the Back Seat" had its
world premiere as part of Summerplay 2016 at
Changing Scene Theatre Northwest in Bremerton, Washington.)*

CHARACTERS
MEG and BEN, brother and sister
Though ages 10 and 14, respectively, they can be played by adults

SET REQUIREMENTS
A bench or two chairs representing the back seat of a car

The time: *Any time at all.*

The place: *The back seat of the family car, represented by a bench or two folding chairs. The stage is otherwise bare.*

At rise, MEG sits in the stage-left chair. BEN sits in the stage-right chair.

MEG gazes out of the "car window" to her left. BEN is occupied with a game on his cell phone, pressing buttons. A second passes. Smiling, MEG raises her hand and waves. BEN seemingly pays no attention. Another few seconds pass. MEG repeats the gesture and the smile.

BEN. *(without looking up from his game)* What're you doing, Toad?

MEG, meanwhile, smiles and waves a third time.

MEG. I'm waving at the cars that go by.

BEN. Why?

MEG. To see if anybody will wave back.

BEN. You're kidding, right?

MEG does not answer. She smiles and waves at another passing car.

Finally BEN looks up from his game. He stares at MEG.

BEN. You are such an unbelievable dork. People probably think you're an idiot.

MEG. So far, nine people have waved back. And I've only been doing it a little while.

BEN. They don't want to hurt the little idiot girl's feelings, is all.

MEG. *(talking to an unseen person in the "front seat")* Dad? Ben just called me an idiot!

BEN. *(also talking to the front seat)* I didn't call her an idiot! I said that people *think* she's an idiot. I wasn't… I didn't… *(pause; to MEG)* Fine. Play your stupid game.

Sulking, BEN returns to his phone game.

A second passes. MEG smiles and waves again.

MEG. Ten.

BEN. Just be quiet. I'm concentrating.

A second passes. MEG smiles and waves.

MEG. *(smugly)* Eleven.

BEN grimaces, but does not look up from his game.

Another second passes. MEG smiles and waves.

Then, crestfallen, she lowers her hand to her lap. No one has waved back this time.

BEN. *(barely glancing up)* Ha.
MEG. You're just jealous.
BEN. Of *you?* Yeah, right.
MEG. You just know that not as many people would wave back at *you.*
BEN. Like I care if a bunch of people I don't even know wave at me. I've got more important things to do.

BEN focuses on playing his game. MEG watches him for just a second or so, and then faces left once more. She raises her hand and waves.

She utters a delighted little laugh.

MEG. There was a big dog in that car.
BEN. *(not looking up from his game)* Did it wave?
MEG. You think you're so smart.
BEN. *(not looking up)* Smarter than you.

BEN smirks as he continues to play his game.

MEG pouts for a moment, then refocuses her attention on looking out the window. A second passes, and she waves. Then she lowers her arm dejectedly. No one waved back. BEN looks at her.

BEN. I guess your winning streak is over. Maybe you're starting to outgrow your cuteness. People don't want to wave at you anymore.

MEG starts to bristle indignantly at this. But after a moment, she reconsiders and chooses another tack.

MEG. You think I'm cute.

BEN looks up from his game, alarmed. He did not expect this.

BEN. I didn't say that.

MEG. You said I *was* cute. *(in a sing-song voice)* You thought I was cu-ute! You thought I was cu-ute!

BEN. I never thought you were cute! What I meant was, other people thought you were.

MEG. *(continuing to chant in a sing-song voice)* You thought I was cu-ute! Ben thought I was cu-ute!

BEN. Quit it! Knock it off!

A moment of silence passes, during which MEG feels very pleased with herself. She looks over at BEN.

MEG. We should have a contest. I bet… I bet that if each of us waved at a bunch of cars, more people would wave back at me than would wave at you.

BEN. *(focused on his game)* We'll never know, will we?

MEG studies BEN for a few seconds. When he pays no attention to her, she sighs and goes back to gazing out the window to her left.

A few more seconds pass. BEN does not look up from his game when he begins to speak.

BEN. Anyway… Of course more cars would wave at you. You're sitting on the side where they're all coming from. Nobody can even see me over here.

Beat.

MEG. *(smugly)* Plus… I'm cute.

BEN. You're a pain, is what you are.

MEG *continues to look out the window to her left. BEN plays his phone game another few seconds, then abruptly shoves the phone into his shirt pocket. He faces MEG.*

BEN. Okay: this is how this is going to work. We each take a turn sitting by that window. We'll each get to wave at ten—no, *twenty*—cars, and see how many wave back. Got it?
MEG. Okay.
BEN. You go first.
MEG. No, I've already been waving. You have to go first.
BEN. *(deep sigh of exasperation)* Fine.

BEN mimes unbuckling his "seat belt."

BEN. Scoot over.

MEG unbuckles her seat belt, and with difficulty, they trade places, BEN crawling clumsily over MEG.

MEG. Ow! *Ow!*
BEN. Oh, be quiet. You're the one who wanted to do this.
MEG. You're squishing me!
BEN. Well, then, *move!* How can I sit there if you're not going to get out of the way?

All of this is spoken as they struggle to change places. At last, they have traded places. Each buckles themselves into their seat belts.

MEG watches BEN. Now that he's in place, BEN is suddenly feeling self-conscious. He looks out the window to his left.

MEG. Okay...

A few seconds pass. BEN continues to look out the window and

MEG continues to watch him, leaning toward him so she can spot approaching cars, as well.

MEG. Here comes one.

MEG. *(beat)* Wave! Come on, wave!

BEN does not wave. MEG turns her head upstage, as if to watch the now-departing car. She turns back to BEN.

MEG. Why didn't you wave?
BEN. I… I wasn't ready.
MEG. Here comes another one.

MEG watches as the "car" passes. She turns around to watch it disappear into the distance, then faces BEN once more, incredulous.

MEG. Why aren't you waving?
BEN. I… I just need a minute, okay? I need to think how to do this.
MEG. You just *wave,* is all. You don't have to think about it.
BEN. Just be quiet.
MEG. Okay. But you only have eighteen chances left.
BEN. Huh-uh! I haven't gotten started yet! I still have all twenty.
MEG. Doesn't look to me like you're ever *going* to start.

BEN glares at her angrily, then turns back to the window. He bucks up his courage, lifts his arm and waves awkwardly, wearing a tense, uncomfortable expression, nothing resembling a smile. A second passes. He lowers his arm.

MEG. Okay. *Now* you have nineteen left.
BEN. I can count, Dork-Breath. I don't need you doing it for me.

BEN draws a deep breath and exhales, as if he's preparing for some-

thing big. He clears his throat.

Both of them lean toward the window. Another car is approaching. BEN lifts his hand and waves, a little more confidently. He is almost, but not quite, smiling.

He lowers his hand, crestfallen. MEG wisely does not say anything this time.

BEN glances at MEG, then turns back to the window. He sees another car approaching, screws up his courage, lifts his hand, smiles, and waves, bigger this time. This time, someone waves back.

He looks pleased. Even MEG looks pleased.

MEG. All right! See? You just need to look like you *mean* it. People can tell if you really mean it.
BEN. *(grinning, but feeling self-conscious)* It's embarrassing. I can't believe you've been sitting here doing this all this time.
MEG. You can quit, if you want. We can just declare me the winner.
BEN. Yeah, right.

Another car approaches. BEN leans forward, smiling broadly and grinning. The car passes. He looks startled. MEG gasps, covering her mouth with her hand. BEN turns around watching the retreating "car" through the back window. He faces forward again.

BEN. He flipped me off. That dude flipped me off!

BEN looks at MEG. They both bust out laughing.

BEN. Has anybody done that to you?
MEG. Never.
BEN. 'Cause you're a girl.

MEG. That was so cool!

BEN. Having somebody tell me to *eff-off*? *(considers this for just a second)* It *was*, kind of. That should count for two points! Because it's even better than a wave back.

MEG. No! … We'll give it one point, same as a wave. *(wistfully)* I hope somebody flips me off when it's my turn. I could make a really awful face. Maybe that would help.

BEN. No, that would be cheating. You can't do anything to make them *want* to show you the bird. *(looking to his left)* Oh, here comes another one!

BEN waves again, this time wildly, with a very exaggerated, wide-mouthed grin on his face.

The "car" passes. Both BEN and MEG look just a little bit disappointed.

BEN. Only a wave.

MEG. Okay, that's how many…? *(counting on her fingers)* Five cars so far. Since you started waving at them, that is. …Two didn't wave… Two did… And the other one… well, *you* know. So that's three points.

BEN. I still think the bird should get two points.

MEG. Well, it doesn't.

Another "car" approaches. BEN leans forward and to his left. He smiles and waves, a little less wildly than last time. He lowers his hand.

MEG. Nothing that time. So, three for six. *(looking to her left)* Oh, here come a whole bunch! Get ready!

BEN leans forward. He raises his hand and waves, smiling.

MEG. *(counting the cars as they pass.)* One… Two… Three.

BEN. That first lady was talking on her phone. She didn't even look.

That one shouldn't count. I should get a do-over for her.

MEG. Okay, a do-over. So then that's just two more who didn't wave.

BEN. No, that one guy did. It was just a little one. He just sort of lifted his fingers off the steering wheel and wiggled them.

MEG. I didn't see him do that.

BEN. Well, he did. So that means eight cars so far, and four points.

MEG. You're such a cheater! …Fine.

BEN turns left, facing the window again. When he can't see her, MEG raises her hand toward him, subtly giving him the bird. After a couple of seconds, she lowers her hand again, smiling.

MEG. *Now* it's four points.

BEN. What?

MEG. Nothing.

BEN looks at MEG with some suspicion. She merely smiles back. He goes back to gazing out the window. A few seconds pass.

BEN. It's weird, you know? Looking in people's cars. It makes you think.

MEG. Huh?

BEN smiles and waves at a passing car. He lowers his hand. The driver has not waved back, but BEN doesn't seem disappointed. Instead, he seems somewhat lost in thought.

BEN. It sort of makes you wonder. What they're like. Who they are. If they like the people they're riding around with. If they're… happy where they are. You know?

MEG. *(considers this for a second)* I don't think any of those things. I just wave.

BEN. But don't you even wonder what makes some of them wave back, and some of them not?

MEG. Would *you* wave? I mean, if we weren't already waving because of the game, if you were just sitting there, looking out the window, and a car went by, and somebody in it waved at you, what would you do? Would you wave back?

BEN. Probably not.

MEG. So, why not?

BEN. I don't know. Because it's dumb. Because I'd feel dumb doing it. Like now.

MEG. Would you ever flip them off?

Beat. BEN grins.

BEN. No. I don't think so.

BEN raises his hand, smiles, and waves at another passing car. This driver waves back.

MEG. Okay, that's five.

BEN. So, why did *he* wave, do you think? He didn't look like the kind of guy who would, you know? He looked… well, old, and kind of grumpy.

MEG. *(shrugs)* Maybe that's the kind of person who needs a wave.

BEN turns to look at MEG. He studies her for a second, then turns back to look out the window again.

BEN. He looked a little bit like Pop-Op, didn't you think?

MEG. I don't remember Pop-Op very well.

BEN. I guess not. You were, what…? About four when he died?

MEG. I guess. *(thinks about this)* Was he grouchy? Like that guy?

BEN lifts his hand and waves at another passing car.

BEN. *(shaking his head)* Nah. I didn't think so, anyway. I think it's just that a lot of old people just naturally look grumpy. They don't mean it.

They just can't help themselves. Their faces sag, or something, when they get to be about fifty.

BEN waves again.

MEG experiments with making her face droop a couple of different ways, the corners of her mouth turning down. She uses her hands to pull her facial skin downward.

MEG. I'm never going to let myself get a saggy face.

Now she uses her hands to lift up the skin on her face, stretching it as far as it will go until her face is very distorted.

MEG. *(still holding up her skin)* I'm going to look cheery and nice all the time.

BEN studies MEG as she continues to hold up her skin.

BEN. You should hold your face like that when you wave to people.

MEG releases her skin. She wiggles her jaw back and forth to more or less set things right with her face.

MEG. I think I remember Pop-Op taking me for a walk one time. And getting me ice cream. I think that was him.
BEN. Probably was.
MEG. I wish I'd known him. Better, I mean. And not just because he bought me ice cream.

BEN turns to the window. He raises his hand in a half-hearted wave.

MEG. How many's that?
BEN. I don't know. I thought you were keeping count.

MEG. I was. But then I got distracted.

BEN. *(sighing)* Doesn't matter. I don't want to play anymore.

MEG. But I didn't even get a turn!

BEN. That's okay. You win, all right? You got more people to wave at you before. You're the big winner.

MEG considers this for a few seconds. It isn't a very satisfactory victory.

BEN. How did you ever start doing this in the first place?

MEG. I don't know. Probably I was just looking out the window one time, and saw somebody in another car looking back. Maybe they waved first, and so I did, too. *(beat)* You're right. It's a dumb game. You want to trade seats back?

BEN. I don't care. I'm fine where I am.

He extracts his phone from his pocket to resume playing his game.

For a few seconds, MEG gazes to her right, out of the window on her side.

MEG. Sherry Delfini thinks it's totally lame. She saw me doing it on the bus, once. Waving out the window. I didn't mean to. I mean, I forgot where I was for a minute, and I just did it. *That* was a mistake.

BEN. Who's Sherry Delfini?

MEG. She's this girl. *(sighs)* She saw me, and she asked what I was doing, and I said, "Nothing." And she said, "I saw you! You were waving out the window! Who were you waving at?" And I said, "Nobody," but she made this big deal of it. "Hey, Meg Spencer waves at strangers out the bus window!"

BEN. Why does Sherry Delfini care whether you wave at people out of the bus window or not?

MEG. I don't know. She just does. She thought it was stupid, and I was dumb. Just like you did.

BEN. I didn't say you were dumb.

MEG. You said it was a stupid game.

BEN. It is a stupid game. But that doesn't mean you're dumb. You're just weird, is all.

Beat. MEG isn't particularly reassured by this. BEN continues to play his game. He does not look up when he speaks his next line.

BEN. Sherry Delfini is the one who's dumb, if you ask me. If she doesn't have anything better to do with her life than watch you waving out the window.

Beat.

MEG. I guess I won't any more.

BEN. *(still focusing on his game)* That's probably a good idea. *(beat)* Just flip people off, instead.

MEG looks at BEN, not quite sure how to take this. He does not look up, but he grins. She looks away and grins, as well.

MEG. You're such a dork. You just want to get me in trouble.

BEN does not respond. He grins and continues to play his game. MEG continues to grin.

END OF PLAY

Dinner Out

CHARACTERS

JESS, a young professional, late 20s/early 30s
MEL, Jess's father
KELLI, another young professional, late 20s/early 30s
ROSE, Kelli's mother

SET REQUIREMENTS

Two tables with two chairs at each,
representing two tables in a restaurant

Lights up on two restaurant tables positioned on opposite sides of the stage. Seated at the stage-right table are JESS and MEL. Nearly empty plates sit in front of each of them. Seated at the stage-left table are KELLI and ROSE. They are in the process of finishing up their meals. Conversation alternates between the occupants at each table, and until the end, no one from either table acknowledges the presence of those at the other table.

At rise, MEL has opened the folder containing their bill.

JESS. Dad, leave that alone. I told you, this is on me.
MEL. You've tipped too much.
JESS. I've tipped just right. It's twenty percent.

JESS takes the folder away from MEL and puts it to the side of her plate.

MEL. Yeah, but our waiter is from one of those Third-World countries. You don't have to tip them as much.

JESS. *(glancing around anxiously; in a hushed tone)* Dad! That's a terrible thing to say!

MEL. I don't mean anything by it. I'm just saying they can get by on a lot less. If anything, I admire them for it. They've learned to be a lot more thrifty.

JESS. You don't tip according to someone's ethnicity.

MEL. You're going to spoil this guy, is all I'm saying. He's going to expect that kind of a tip from everybody, now.

JESS. Please, just drink your coffee and let me worry about the bill.

MEL shrugs and lifts his cup to take a sip.

ROSE. *(glancing around)* This place is just lovely, Kelli. This is just so nice of you.

KELLI. I'm glad you're enjoying yourself, Ma.

ROSE. I am. This fish is just delicious. I almost never make fish at home anymore. It seems like so much trouble.

KELLI. That's funny.

ROSE. What is?

KELLI. Well, it seemed like we had fish a couple of times a week when we were kids. Roger and I used to complain because you served it so often. And you'd say, "Fish is brain food. You want to be dumb when you grow up?"

ROSE. So, see? Thanks to me, you're not. I'm not so sure about your brother, though.

KELLI. *(laughing)* Ma…

JESS. How are you liking the new apartment?

MEL. It's good. It's a hell of a lot easier to clean, I'll tell you.

JESS. Any potential buyers on the house?

MEL. *(shrugging)* I'm in no hurry.

JESS. Well, it's a seller's market right now. You could probably name your price and get what you want for it.

MEL. *(chuckles)* What do you know about sellers' markets, little girl? You think you're a realtor or something?

ROSE. You can bet it would never occur to Roger to do something like this for me. You got all the thoughtfulness, that's for sure.

KELLI. He's just real busy right now, Ma. That doesn't mean he doesn't care.

ROSE. See? That's what I mean. Finding excuses for him. That's just you. Your brother could find the time, you know. Being married doesn't make a person busy.

KELLI. I was talking about his job.

ROSE. But that Carol. She demands so much attention, it's no wonder.

KELLI. *(trying to change the subject)* So, did you save room for dessert? They have some decadent things here.

JESS. I'm just saying that unless you're planning to rent it out, it seems kind of a waste to be paying property taxes and insurance on something that's just going to sit there unoccupied for who knows how long.

MEL. I don't want to be a landlord. Just a bunch of headaches. I don't want to go chasing after rent every month. And tenants can always find something wrong with a place, no matter how nice it is. Plus, you don't know what kind of people might show up.

JESS. Fine. It's your house. I guess you can do whatever you want.

MEL. Maybe you'd move back there some day. When you've got a family. It's a great neighborhood to raise kids in.

JESS. You want more coffee? I wouldn't mind a little more.

MEL. Nah, I'm good.

ROSE. Did I tell you what that Carol said to me last week?

KELLI. I don't know. And why do you call her "that Carol?" Right away, I know it means you've got a beef with her about something.

ROSE. She's got an opinion about everything. And she's not afraid to share it.

KELLI. *(smiling)* And who wants to be around someone like that?

ROSE. That's a crack; you think I don't know that's a crack?

KELLI. I'm just saying, she loves Roger and he loves her. He thinks she hung the moon. Isn't that enough?

MEL. How's work these days?

JESS. It's good. Real good, in fact. They've assigned me a new project—

MEL. —I hope they're paying you a little better.

ROSE. She gets so snippy, is what I was going to say. You can't make even a little suggestion without her getting defensive. I didn't realize that when your son gets married, you give up the right to make even a suggestion.

JESS. They're paying me fine, Dad. In fact, I'll probably be getting a bonus based on last quarter's review.

MEL. About time. I never understood why you accepted that job in the first place. Not at those wages.

JESS. I was just out of college. I didn't have a track record, and remember, the economy wasn't exactly conducive to finding work.

KELLI. I've heard your little suggestions, Ma. All my life I've heard them. *(with slight sarcasm)* Carol's new to the experience. She doesn't realize they're given with love.

MEL. Have you ever once asked for a raise? How long have you been there now?

JESS. I just told you, Dad, I'm in line for a bonus.

MEL. I'll take that as a No, then. You should show a little backbone, Jess. A good employer appreciates that.

ROSE. And anyway, I don't know why you're always so quick to defend her. You think Roger isn't always taking her side?

KELLI. I'm just saying—

ROSE. —And it's not like she doesn't take her little swipes at you, too, now and then. You may think she's Little Miss Perfect, but she does not extend the same courtesy to you.

KELLI. I don't want to hear this, Ma.

MEL. You know what I always say: "How can you expect somebody else…"

MEL and JESS finish the rest of the speech in unison.

MEL/JESS. "…to respect you, if you don't respect yourself?"
JESS. I respect myself, Dad. Of course I do.

MEL shrugs skeptically.

ROSE. For one thing, she alludes to your lack of fashion sense.
KELLI. How about the chocolate cake? They make an amazing flour-less chocolate cake.
ROSE. She was talking about your classic style, and how distinctive she thinks you look.
KELLI. And how is that a "swipe?"
ROSE. "Classic," Kelli. She's saying you dress old-fashioned.
KELLI. *(amused)* I don't think that's necessarily what she's saying.
ROSE. Those little back-handed compliments… you have to watch out for those.
MEL. So… what about that Phil guy?
JESS. Phil?
MEL. That guy you've been seeing?
JESS. Phil Evans? Jeez, Dad, that was awhile ago. Nearly two years.
MEL. So, you're not seeing him any more?
JESS. No.
KELLI. I'm thinking I might try the cheesecake.
ROSE. Oh, and that's another thing… She hinted around that maybe it wouldn't hurt if you dropped a pound or two.
KELLI. Did she, Ma? Did she really? Because that sounds a little more like something I've heard from you once or twice.
ROSE. So, I'm the enemy, now?
KELLI. Nobody's the enemy. But I find it pretty hard—no, impossible—to believe that Carol offered up an unsolicited opinion about my weight.
ROSE. Well… I might have mentioned a little something when we

were on the phone the other night. How I'm just a little concerned… and she didn't rush to correct me. Didn't exactly come to your defense.

MEL. So, who are you seeing these days? Anybody?

JESS. Dad…

MEL. I know, I know, it's none of my business.

JESS. No, it's not that at all. Of course it's your business. It's your business a *little* bit. I'm just always hesitant to bring it up.

MEL. …Ah, so there *is* someone.

JESS. …Maybe.

KELLI. Ma, you *are* aware that Carol and I talk to each other now and then? We have a chance to compare notes?

ROSE. Oh… So the two of you are talking behind my back, is that it?

KELLI. Why is it you think anybody has to be talking behind anybody's back? I'm just saying Carol and I are friendly.

ROSE. Friendly.

KELLI. Yes.

JESS. But I know how you get. You weren't exactly friendly toward Phil.

MEL. I wouldn't say that.

JESS. I would. And he did.

MEL. Oh he did, did he? The little weasel.

JESS. My point. It's difficult to introduce anybody to you, anybody who, you know, might be special to me. You go into Overprotective Father Mode at the drop of a hat.

MEL. Can I help it if I care? Can I help it if my little girl means the world to me?

JESS. And I wouldn't want it any other way. *(beat)* Well, I might want it a slightly different way. I love you for it, Dad, but you have some pretty exacting standards.

MEL. Which you ought to have for yourself. And I can't say I've seen you demonstrate a lot of those.

JESS. Just because mine may not match up exactly with yours does not make them less valid.

MEL. *(snorting derisively)* "Less valid."

ROSE. So what is it you and that Carol… *(pausing to correct herself)* What is it you… and *Carol* find so much to talk about?

KELLI. I never said we have a lot to talk about, Ma. I'm just saying we do talk. We're sisters-in-law. Of course we talk. And I like her. I think she's a nice person, and I think she's wonderful to Roger.

ROSE. Well. Isn't that nice.

KELLI. It *is* nice, Ma. And you should be happy. You've raised two kids who love you, and who are out there living productive, fulfilling lives. Your son has found a terrific woman to share his with.

ROSE. *(solemnly)* Of course I'm happy. Who said I'm not happy?

KELLI. So… at the risk of getting even fatter than I already am, how about we have dessert?

ROSE. *(warming slightly)* You're not fat, Kelli. Nobody said you were fat. I don't know where you get that.

ROSE sets her napkin on the table.

ROSE. I need to visit the ladies room. Get me a tea if the waiter comes by.

ROSE stands and exits left.

MEL. So, who is this new Mister Wonderful in your life?

JESS. See, it's when you take that tone, Dad, that the alarm bells start to go off. You've already made up your mind. You've set yourself up for certain expectations.

MEL. Not true. I'm excited for you.

JESS. Well, we'll see about that. Anyway, yes, there might be someone. It's… it's a little early to say. But it's somebody my friend Carol introduced me to. In fact, there's a reason I decided to bring you here today.

MEL. As long as he's not a bum, I'll be fine with it.

JESS. He's not a bum, Dad. In fact, he's not even a—

MEL. —And maybe not from the south. Phil was from Georgia, wasn't he? I'd just as soon not have any redneck, gap-toothed grandkids. But other than that, I'd be fine with just about anybody you wanted to date, sweetheart.

MEL raises his mug to take another gulp of coffee. As he does so, JESS turns and looks over her shoulder at KELLI, who is looking at her. JESS shakes her head "no." KELLI nods sadly in agreement. JESS turns back to the table. MEL lowers his cup to the table.

MEL. Well?
JESS. Well nothing, Dad. There's nobody I want you to meet. Not yet.
MEL. That's okay, Jessica. There will be someday.
JESS. Maybe, Dad. Maybe someday.

The lights fade.

END OF PLAY

A Last Behest

CHARACTERS

EDGAR (70s), a dying man
WINSTON (30s/40s), his long-suffering attorney
MS. WEEDEMAYER (30s/40s), his mousy-but-loyal secretary
RAMONA (50s), Edgar's daughter; rather unpleasant
ARTHUR (50s), Ramona's husband
GARRETT (late 20s/30s), Edgar's chauffeur; an opportunist
PHILIPPA (late 20s), Edgar's granddaughter; a bit of a floozy
STUART (mid to late 20s), Edgar's grandson; an uncertain young man

SET REQUIREMENTS

*Edgar's bedroom can be elaborate, or as simple
as a cot, a small table and a handful of chairs*

Scene: EDGAR ROBELARD's bedroom.

*At rise, EDGAR, an elderly man, reposes in his bed, center, eyes
closed. His attorney WINSTON, an officious-looking man in a dark
suit and glasses, sits in a chair to the stage right+ of the bed. He holds
a folder in his lap.*

WINSTON. You're absolutely certain this is how you want to do this,
Edgar?

EDGAR nods without opening his eyes.

WINSTON. And you feel you're up for it just now?

EDGAR nods again and waves one hand impatiently.

WINSTON. I understand. I just can't help but feel this is somewhat ill-advised. No, no, I understand. It's none of my damn business, I'm just your attorney, I'm not paid to make suggestions, I'm paid to carry out your requests, you've made that perfectly—and repeatedly—clear.

EDGAR nods.

WINSTON. *(sighing heavily)* Fine. You were a full-blown eccentric when you were hale and hearty, and now that you're on your dea… Well, now that you are where you are now… you've only gone further round the bend. With your permission, I'm at least going to fortify myself first.

> *EDGAR flicks his fingers in the direction of the small table containing a brandy decanter and snifters.*

> *WINSTON crosses to the table and pours himself a small amount, swirls it in the glass and downs it in a single gulp.*

WINSTON. *(clearing his throat)* Let's do this thing, then.

> *WINSTON crosses to a closed door. He opens it and leans out.*

WINSTON. *(raising his voice slightly)* All right, if you'd all care to step inside…

> *WINSTON steps back from the open doorway to allow a parade of people to enter. They are RAMONA and ARTHUR (both 50s-60s), MS. WEEDEMAYER (30s-40s), STUART, PHILIPPA and GARRETT (all 20s–early 30s). They all takes seats on the stage-left side of the room, apart from RAMONA, who rushes to EDGAR's bedside. PHILIPPA and GARRETT, meanwhile, exchange a few subtle, flirta-*

tious looks throughout the following proceedings.

RAMONA. Oh, Father! Father, what is this all about?

EDGAR raises one hand as if to hold her off.

WINSTON. Mrs. Claremore, if you please.
RAMONA. This is my father, dammit! What kind of shenanigans are you pulling here?
WINSTON. None of this is my idea, I assure you. Your father wanted to have a few words with each member of the household before… well… *(clearing his throat)* at any rate, if you would rejoin the others, Mrs. Claremore, we'll get things started.

RAMONA crosses and sits with the others. WINSTON crosses to stand in front of his chair. He opens a folder and begins to read.

WINSTON. Mr. Robelard has a few things he wishes to say to each of you in turn. If each of you would step to his bedside when I summon you, he will do his best to communicate. As you know, his strength is waning and his voice very weak, so you will need to lean close in order to hear what he has to say. But first, he has asked that I read a prepared statement.

WINSTON adjusts his glasses and clears his throat once more.

WINSTON. "My dear family, my kind friends, my treasured employees. As my time on this mortal coil draws to an end, I thought I should disclose a few things I've held close to my vest until now. Some of these will cause delight, others will perplex. Some you may have guessed at already, some may come as a complete surprise. Please, indulge an old man and allow him this opportunity to achieve closure and to pass from this life into the next with his conscience unburdened. I believe that when all is told, each and every one of you will leave this room with your lives changed in some meaningful way."

WINSTON closes the folder. General murmurs of interest and uneasiness among the gathered group.

WINSTON. Mr. Robelard's trusted secretary, Ms. Weedemayer.

The prim, timid, conservatively dressed MS. WEEDEMAYER steps forward, crossing to stand near the foot of EDGAR's bed. EDGAR raises one arm, beckoning her with a crooked finger.

WINSTON. Do not be shy. Step forward, please. And bend down so that Mr. Robelard doesn't have to exert himself.

MS. WEEDEMAYER steps close and bends down so that her ear is by EDGAR's face. He speaks very softly into her ear.

As he speaks, her face goes through a variety of expressions. She has a series of audible intakes of breath after each thing EDGAR whispers.

She gasps and clutches her bosom, looking shocked.

She gasps again and glances over her shoulder at the rest of the group. She smiles slightly, causing everyone else to shift uncomfortably.

She gasps again and giggles.

She gasps again and bites her knuckles.

She nods vigorously and takes a few steps back from the bed.

MS. WEEDEMAYER. I understand, sir. Thank you.

She takes a moment to compose herself with a newfound confidence she clearly has never had before. Gone is the meek, mousy secretary. Now she is a sleek, confident, sultry individual. She turns on her heels and marches across the room to the door. Before leaving, she pauses to look over each person standing there in a haughty, dismissive way.

She shakes her head, utters a small, scornful laugh, and exits with flourish. The others watch her go and then glance uncomfortably at one another.

WINSTON. Mr. Robelard's son-in-law, Arthur Claremore.

ARTHUR, a somewhat overstuffed, overly dignified man steps forward. He is trying to move with confidence, but a certain amount of nervousness shows through his bravado.

ARTHUR. *(boisterously)* Hello, Edgar. You're looking well. Well, all things considered, given your current—

EDGAR reaches up to take hold of ARTHUR's necktie and yanks his head down so that his ear is near EDGAR's mouth.

ARTHUR. Oh! Um, well…

EDGAR begins whispering into ARTHUR's ear.

ARTHUR. *(listening)* Uh-huh…Yes… She *what?*

ARTHUR's eyes widen. He starts to straighten up, but EDGAR still has hold of his necktie and pulls him down again.

ARTHUR. Are you telling me… …I… but… Oh. I see.

EDGAR releases ARTHUR's tie. ARTHUR straightens. He adjusts his tie and the rest of his appearance. He moves with precise dignity, crossing to look coldly at RAMONA.

ARTHUR. I won't be bothering you further, Ramona. Rest assured.
RAMONA. What? Bother me? Whatever are you talking about, darling?

ARTHUR looks at STUART.

ARTHUR. Stuart…
STUART. Pop?
ARTHUR. At least, now I know *why* you've always been a disappointment. It comes as a bit of a relief, actually.

ARTHUR exits with as much dignified flair as he can muster.

RAMONA. *(watching him go)* Arthur? Arthur, where are you going? *(to EDGAR)* Father? What did you say to him? *(in general)* What in heaven's name is going on here?
WINSTON. Mr. Robelard's chauffeur and valet, Garrett Waymire.

GARRETT disentangles himself from PHILIPPA, standing and crossing to bend down in front of EDGAR.

He listens for a second or so, but EDGAR doesn't say anything. Puzzled, GARRETT straightens up. He looks at WINSTON, who gestures that he should bend down again.

As GARRETT bends down, EDGAR raises his hand and slaps GARRETT across the face. GARRETT straightens, touching his hand to his freshly slapped cheek, looking somewhat bewildered.

WINSTON. *(to GARRETT)* That's it. That's all he had to say. You may take your seat again. ...Mr. Robelard's granddaughter, Philippa Claremore.

PHILIPPA rises and crosses as GARRETT returns to his seat. As they meet in passing, she pauses to caress his cheek.

PHILIPPA. Poor baby.

PHILIPPA bends down over EDGAR, her ear above his face. EDGAR murmurs into her ear.

PHILIPPA. Hello, Grandfather... Uh-huh. ...Yes. ...No. *(glancing at GARRETT)* ...Of course he does. ...No. No! There's nothing you could say that would... would...

PHILIPPA stands up slowly. She blinks a few times, then turns and crosses back to the others.

PHILIPPA. *(looking at RAMONA; coldly)* Mother. *(looking at GARRETT; coldly)* Garrett. I hope you'll be very happy together.

PHILIPPA crosses to leave, then returns long enough to deliver a slap to GARRETT's face before turning on her heel and stalking out. Again, GARRETT touches his bruised cheek, bewildered.

RAMONA. Philippa? Darling? What is it? Come back here!
GARRETT. Philippa? Wait! Wait up! What did he tell you?

RAMONA and GARRETT both exit hastily in pursuit of PHILIPPA.

WINSTON. *(to STUART)* Mr. Robelard's grandson, Stuart Claremore.

STUART stands and crosses to stand next to EDGAR.

STUART. *(to WINSTON)* He… He isn't going to hit me, is he?

WINSTON shrugs. With some misgivings, STUART bends down, his ear just above EDGAR's face. EDGAR murmurs in his ear.

STUART. Grandfather? …Well, um… yes. Yes, I… I… what?

STUART raises his head a few inches and looks down at EDGAR. EDGAR feebly beckons that STUART should listen some more, and STUART again lowers his ear to above EDGAR's face.

STUART. Are… are you sure? …Really? …You… you think I should?

EDGAR nods.

STUART straightens. He crosses to WINSTON.

STUART. I… Grandfather said… Well, I never dared hope, but…

STUART looks over his shoulder at EDGAR, who, without opening his eyes or lifting his head, raises his hand in a "go ahead" sort of gesture.

STUART faces WINSTON once more, takes a deep breath, raises his hands to WINSTON's face and pulls him close and kisses him.

After a few seconds, the folder in WINSTON's hand falls to the floor, scattering papers everywhere.

STUART ends the kiss, releasing his grip on WINSTON's face, and takes a step back. WINSTON's hair and coat are thoroughly mussed.

STUART. I… I guess I'll be seeing you later, then.

He smiles shyly at WINSTON, then turns and crosses left, exiting.

WINSTON blinks several times. Primly, he adjusts his glasses, collar and coat and smooths his hair. He bends down to pick up the scattered pages. Once they are back in the folder, he crosses to the door. He clears his throat.

WINSTON. *(calling through the doorway)* Mrs. Claremore…? Are you still out there? Would you come back in, please.

After some delay, RAMONA scurries in, clearly agitated.

RAMONA. I just don't understand what's happened.

RAMONA crosses to EDGAR's bed.

RAMONA. Father? What have you been telling everyone? What is going on here?

EDGAR beckons, and she bends down so that her ear is above his face. He murmurs in her ear.

RAMONA. What? Oh, but no… Well, yes, but… but there's *Arthur*, after all!

RAMONA raises her face to look at WINSTON, who returns the look with misgivings. He takes a step back.

RAMONA. No… Well, I can't say I hadn't thought about it, but still… No. No, I couldn't possibly.

RAMONA straightens. She clasps EDGAR's hand for a moment, then releases it. Summoning her courage, she crosses to stand in front of WINSTON.

RAMONA. My father has alerted me to your feelings. And, while I cannot say that I'm not flattered, the simple truth is that I took a vow, and I intend to live up to it. I hope you understand.

WINSTON. Uh… certainly.

RAMONA nods in a most dignified way. She turns away and takes just a step or two before whirling back and, as STUART did before her, lunges at WINSTON, capturing his face in her hands and kissing him passionately. Once again, WINSTON drops his folder, spilling pages all over the floor. The kiss lasts several seconds and then RAMONA releases him, taking a step back.

RAMONA. *(studying WINSTON a second longer)* Well, then. I just wanted to see what I might have missed out on. …Hm. Pity.

RAMONA turns, touching her hair delicately, and crosses left and exits. WINSTON watches her go. RAMONA's lipstick is smeared generously across his mouth, and she has wildly mussed his hair. Only after she has gone does he adjust his tie and glasses.

WINSTON. Well, that's everyone, then.

WINSTON takes out a handkerchief and dabs his lips.

WINSTON. You do love your little jokes, don't you, Edgar?

EDGAR smiles without opening his eyes. WINSTON kneels to pick up his papers once more as the lights fade.

END OF PLAY

The Kitchen Fairy

*("The Kitchen Fairy" had its premiere in March 2017
at Theatre Three on Long Island, New York.)*

CHARACTERS

LONNIE (30s–up), office supervisor
CAITLYN (20s–up), office worker

SET REQUIREMENTS

LONNIE's desk, two chairs

CAITLYN enters. LONNIE is seated at his desk.

CAITLYN. We need to talk.
LONNIE. Are you dying?
CAITLYN. No.
LONNIE. Are you sick?
CAITLYN. No.
LONNIE. Are you quitting?
CAITLYN. No.
LONNIE. Then we don't need to talk. Not right now.
CAITLYN. We do, Lonnie. We do.
LONNIE. *(sighing heavily)* Caitlyn, do you know how many conversations you begin with those words?
CAITLYN. I wouldn't say it if—
LONNIE/CAITLYN. *(unison)* —it wasn't important.

LONNIE. Yeah, yeah. The thing is, everything can't be of equal impor-
tance, can it?

CAITLYN. I know—

LONNIE/CAITLYN. *(unison)* —but this is.

LONNIE. Doesn't it tell you anything when I can finish so many of
your sentences for you? Doesn't it sort of paint a picture?

CAITLYN. You've always said you have an open-door policy.

LONNIE. I know—

CAITLYN. —You've always said we can come to you if there's a problem.

LONNIE. Yes, I have. And every now and then, I regret it.

*CAITLYN regards LONNIE solemnly. A few seconds pass. He sighs,
giving in.*

LONNIE. All right. Tell me what's bothering you.

*CAITLYN takes a seat in the chair opposite LONNIE's desk. She waits
just a second before delivering her message to build up the import.*

CAITLYN. People are leaving their dirty coffee cups stacked in the
sink in the break room.

LONNIE slumps forward, resting his head in his hands in exasperation.

LONNIE. *(muttering to himself)* I knew it.

CAITLYN. Despite the fact that there's a sign posted right over the
counter.

LONNIE. Caitlyn…

CAITLYN. Right there! It says, "Please do not leave dirty dishes lying
around. Please clean up after yourselves." And people are just ignoring it!

LONNIE. Caitlyn…

CAITLYN. And do you know what's worse?

LONNIE. See, this is the kind of thing that—

CAITLYN. —Somebody wrote some nasty little comment, in teeny tiny letters down in one corner of my sign. I'm not even going to tell you what they said, because that's not the point. They were mocking me, that's the point!

LONNIE. Dishes.

CAITLYN. Yes! Dirty dishes! It's just so disrespectful!

LONNIE. Let me try to put this into perspective for you. I am putting the finishing touches on a proposal that, if accepted, could net our company a significant amount of money. And it needs to go out of here before five o'clock this evening. I really need to stay focused, Caitlyn. I can't afford any distractions, not right now.

CAITLYN. So, that's what I am? A distraction?

LONNIE. If it comes down to coffee cups in a sink versus a half-million dollar deal, then, yes. I'm sorry, but yes.

CAITLYN. Someone defaced my sign!

LONNIE. And that was rude. They shouldn't have done that. We can talk about it later. First thing tomorrow, maybe.

CAITLYN. I don't want to talk about it. I want somebody to do something about it.

LONNIE. How about for right now, you make a new sign? And laminate it. That way, nobody will be able to write on it.

CAITLYN. But that's just admitting defeat. That's just *upping my game,* which is going to invite them to do the same. They'll just find something else to do to it, instead.

LONNIE. Well, then, what did you have in mind?

CAITLYN. Something that sends a clear message: that there will be repercussions if you can't be bothered to clean up after yourself. Like some rat poison sprinkled in the coffee.

LONNIE stares at CAITLYN for several seconds. Then he laughs. CAITLYN smiles, as well.

LONNIE. Yeah, that would certainly teach them.

CAITLYN. I don't mean enough to, you know, *kill* them. Just enough to make them think about what they've done. While they're squirming and sweating.

LONNIE stops laughing. Now he's a little concerned.

LONNIE. It's a great fantasy, of course. But you can't really do that.
CAITLYN. Can't you?
LONNIE. No, you can't.
CAITLYN. I think what you're saying is… "You maybe shouldn't."
LONNIE. No… I'm saying you definitely shouldn't. And you can't.
CAITLYN. *(considering this for a second)* Oh. Hm.

CAITLYN stands.

CAITLYN. Well, I'll let you get back to your proposal.

CAITLYN turns to leave.

LONNIE. Caitlyn?

CAITLYN turns back to look at LONNIE. A couple of seconds pass.

LONNIE. Never mind.

CAITLYN turns back again to leave. She gets a few steps closer to the door.

LONNIE. Caitlyn?

CAITLYN turns back again and looks at LONNIE once more.

LONNIE. You were joking, right? …You wouldn't really… I mean…

rat poison? In the coffee pot?

CAITLYN. Of course not, Lonnie. That would just be so wrong.

LONNIE is enormously relieved.

LONNIE. I figured you were joking… I mean, I *knew* you were joking, but I had to ask, right?

CAITLYN. Not in the coffee pot. That wouldn't be fair to the others.

LONNIE. "The others?"

CAITLYN. Not everybody leaves their dirty dishes in the sink. Why should they be punished?

LONNIE. Then… how…?

CAITLYN. *(smugly)* Oh, I keep a watch. I know who takes their cups in there and just leaves them. The ones who think there's some kind of a kitchen fairy who washes everybody's nasty old dishes and keeps the place neat and tidy. Well, that kitchen fairy also knows when people step away from their desk during the day and leave their coffee un-guarded for a few minutes. That's how to do it. That way, it happens to all the right people.

Beat. LONNIE can't help but look at the coffee cup sitting on his own desk.

LONNIE. But… you wouldn't… You've never actually done that…?

CAITLYN. *(musing to herself)* Entitlement. That's what it is. People who've arrived at the notion that, somehow, the ordinary rules don't apply to them. They're *too good* to wash their own dishes. They can't be *bothered* to use their turn signals. *So what* if there's a handicapped parking sign? They're only going to be in the store for a few minutes. And they don't have *that many* more than fifteen items when they go through the express checkout. Nobody's going to tell *them* they need to silence their cell phone during the show. Somebody *else* can put paper in the copier when the tray's empty.

LONNIE. Caitlyn..?

CAITLYN. Oh, the list goes on and on.

LONNIE. Caitlyn, I need you to tell me: did you put rat poison in anybody's coffee?

The question snaps CAITLYN back to the moment. She looks at LONNIE.

CAITLYN. It was just a passing comment, Lonnie. You asked, remember? You asked what I thought we should do about people and their dirty dishes. I offered up my opinion.

LONNIE. So… no…?

CAITLYN. No.

LONNIE. *(relieved)* All right.

CAITLYN. There are a lot of ways to get your point across, after all. Someone walks out to find they've got a flat tire, not once, but a couple of times, always on the same day they took something from the refrigerator that had somebody else's name on it… eventually, they put two and two together.

LONNIE. Pam had two flat tires last month. In the same week.

CAITLYN. And you notice how nobody's pudding cups have gone missing lately?

LONNIE. Are you telling me…?

CAITLYN. Karma, Lonnie. That's what I'm telling you. Karma.

LONNIE. You… You had a disagreement with Tony a while ago, didn't you?

CAITLYN. *(nodding)* He was deliberately taking up two spaces in the parking lot. So that nobody would ding the sides of his precious new car. "At least park at the far end of the lot if you're going to do that," I told him. He just laughed.

LONNIE. And then… he had that accident.

CAITLYN. Oh, that's right… Took a tumble down a flight of stairs, didn't he?

LONNIE. He said there was something slippery on the landing. We figured the janitorial staff had left some water or soap there after mopping.

CAITLYN. Gosh, so sad. It's fortunate he wasn't hurt worse than he was. On the bright side, he can use a handicapped space until he's off those crutches.

LONNIE. There was that time Susan got trapped in the elevator. She'd been working late, so nobody else was in the building. She was there all night.

CAITLYN. Don't elevators have those emergency phones in them?

LONNIE. It wasn't working, for some reason. …Had you and Susan had any kind of a conflict?

CAITLYN. Not that I recall …offhand.

LONNIE regards CAITLYN dubiously for a few seconds.

CAITLYN. Oh, honestly, Lonnie. Do you think I have the knowledge or the capability of disabling an elevator?

LONNIE. To be honest, I am starting to wonder what you're capable of.

CAITLYN. *(musing; a faraway look in her eyes)* So many injustices, every day, every place you look. It's depressing.

LONNIE. It's true, I know. And… And that's why we have to let a lot of them just go by. Otherwise, how would we ever accomplish anything? You see what I'm saying, Caitlyn? We can't let ourselves get too worked up over some coffee cups in the sink.

CAITLYN. What about the bigger things, Lonnie? What about those?

LONNIE. I guess that depends. You aren't talking about pudding cups again, are you?

CAITLYN. I'm talking about screwing someone over for a promotion. I'm talking about getting a person fired.

LONNIE. Who… Who did that?

CAITLYN. You remember Phil Parsons?

LONNIE. Phil?

CAITLYN. You remember Tina Edgewater?

LONNIE. Tina? Sure. …Wait… Are you saying Phil…?

CAITLYN. It's pretty easy to make a person look bad… look *incompetent* in front of their co-workers, their bosses. A few messages that somehow don't get delivered. Somebody doesn't find out that an important meeting has been rescheduled to an earlier time. And if you can get hold of someone's password, you can cause all kinds of damage.

LONNIE. No… Now I've known Phil a long time, and he wouldn't—

CAITLYN. —And poor Tina. *(laughs softly)* You know, there was a time I couldn't have imagined those words would pass my lips: "Poor Tina." So young, and so pretty. Everybody liked her. And yet so insecure. So when a nice-looking man started paying attention to her, she fell right into his arms. For a while, it was all starlight and soft music and wonderful. Until she started being too needy, too clingy. Then she'd become something of a problem. And, all of a sudden, her quarterly review reflected a real downturn in performance.

LONNIE. Caitlyn, where is all of this going?

CAITLYN. Finally it was suggested she seek employment elsewhere. And I couldn't even bring myself to feel sorry for the little twit because she was still so in love with the bastard that she wouldn't say anything.

LONNIE. You want revenge on her behalf, is that it?

CAITLYN. No, not at all. If she isn't bold enough—or smart enough—to stand up for herself, she deserves what she gets.

LONNIE. Because Phil dumped her.

CAITLYN. Phil didn't dump her, Lonnie. *You* did. You screwed *both* of them over. One literally, and the other one figuratively. I watched what you did, Lonnie. Somehow, you figured out Phil's password. And then you got into his files, and you changed the figures in that report before he turned it in. Right around the time you were both up for that promotion.

LONNIE. *(amused)* Where are you getting this, Caitlyn? That's crazy.

CAITLYN. You changed them just enough so they looked like careless mistakes. Now, Phil really should have double-checked things before his presentation the next morning and saved himself some embarrassment, so that's on him.

LONNIE. Do you know how difficult it would be to do something like that, without leaving a clear trail right back to myself?

CAITLYN. About as difficult as disabling an elevator, I would imagine. …Now, about Tina. See, she was just so happy about her torrid workplace romance that she had to share the details with someone.

CAITLYN gestures to herself.

LONNIE. So? There's no company policy against co-workers having a relationship.

CAITLYN. Yes. But all those negative comments in her personnel folder, the ones that led to her poor performance review… those all came from you. She was starting to weigh you down, wasn't she, Lonnie?

LONNIE. You have no substantive proof of any of this. Just… Just theories and innuendo.

CAITLYN. And I don't have to tell you how damaging innuendo can be. Do I?

CAITLYN sits.

CAITLYN. You're a bright boy. And ambitious. I think I want to hitch my wagon to yours, 'cause you're going places.

LONNIE. Now I see.

LONNIE stands.

LONNIE. So… If a managerial position opens up, I should recommend you. Or suggest it's time you had a raise.

CAITLYN. Oh, something like that. That report you're working on… *(gesturing to the pages on LONNIE's desk)* You're going to land that half-million dollar deal, I have no doubt. And when you do, they're going to put you in charge of a whole new division. And I want to be there, right at your side. As your executive assistant.

LONNIE. My executive assistant?

CAITLYN. We're alike in a lot of ways, Lonnie. Think of what great things we could accomplish together.

LONNIE. Yeah… And you think I should trust you?

CAITLYN. Oh, not for one minute of one single day. Don't ever leave your coffee—or your back—unguarded. The same way I won't. We're not to be trusted, either one of us. But don't you see how marvelous that will be?

LONNIE. Marvelous?

CAITLYN. We'll keep each other on our toes constantly. Our minds are going to be racing, each trying to keep up with the other, for fear of what might happen, what the other person might do.

CAITLYN stands.

CAITLYN. I'd tell you to take a little time and think about it, but we both know there's not really anything to think about, is there? …Well, I should get back to my desk. I'm sure a lot of those busybodies out there are wondering what we've been doing in here all this time.

CAITLYN turns to leave, then turns back to LONNIE.

CAITLYN. Oh, and I'm serious about those dirty dishes that people leave in the sink. Something has to be done about it. But you don't need to worry about that. *(smiling)* I'll come up with something.

CAITLYN exits. LONNIE watches her go, and then sinks slowly back into his chair as the lights fade.

END OF PLAY

Maybe a Dalmatian

CHARACTERS

ZOEY (30s/40s), a mother-type
WALTER (40s), a father-type
AUNT EILEEN (40s/60s), spinster aunt
JENNY (late teens/20s), a daughter-type
COBEY (late teens/20s), a son-type
ZOEY 2 (8 years old), a younger version of ZOEY
MARGARET (mid 30s/early 40s), ZOEY 2's mother;
an unpleasant woman

SET REQUIREMENTS

A card table, around which are gathered five chairs

Lights up on a nearly bare stage. A small table/card table sits center. Five chairs are positioned around it. One is empty. The other four are occupied by WALTER, AUNT EILEEN, JENNY and COBEY.

In front of each character, as well as in front of the empty chair, is a place setting consisting of a small plastic plate, a spoon and a fork. Each of the four people has a napkin in his/her lap. All are dressed in casual, but nice, clothing, reflecting the style and income level of an upper-middle-class, middle-America family.

At rise, all are sitting perfectly still, each with a benevolent smile on his/her face, each gazing down at the table. They hold these positions for several seconds until ZOEY enters, right.

ZOEY enters, wearing an apron over an attractive dress. She, like AUNT EILEEN, is a pleasant, motherly type. She carries a tray holding five empty small plastic bowls, and crosses to the table where she begins placing a bowl in front of each person. She begins speaking as soon as she enters.

ZOEY. Here we are. I hope everybody's hungry. We're starting off with some vegetable soup. Now, be careful, because it's good and hot.

As soon as a bowl is placed in front of COBEY, he picks up his spoon and dips it into the bowl. ZOEY gently smacks his hand.

ZOEY. Cobey! You wait until everybody has been served.
COBEY. But I'm hungry, just like you said!
ZOEY. That's no excuse for not minding your manners, young man.

ZOEY exits right with the tray.

When she is gone, JENNY sticks her tongue out at COBEY.

JENNY. *(sing-song)* You got in trouble, you got in trouble!
ZOEY. *(off)* I heard that, young lady!

ZOEY re-enters without the tray. She sits in the empty chair.

ZOEY. There will be no teasing your brother.
COBEY. *(to JENNY)* Ha ha!
ZOEY. That goes for you, too, Mister.

ZOEY shakes open her napkin and places it in her lap.

ZOEY. All right, then.

As if this is their cue, everyone picks up their spoon and begins eating their "soup."

WALTER. Oh, well, this is delicious, Honey.
AUNT EILEEN. It is, Zoey. It's marvelous.
ZOEY. Thank you, Aunt Eileen.
WALTER. Just hits the spot.
ZOEY. Not all the spots, I hope. There's more to come.
COBEY. What else are we having?
ZOEY. Chicken and dumplings.

Everyone reacts with favorable sounds.

COBEY. My favorite!
ZOEY. So… how was everyone's day? How was work? How was school?
COBEY. I got an A on my spelling test.
JENNY. I made the cheerleading squad.
ZOEY. Oh, my gosh. Isn't that wonderful! Both of you.
COBEY. And there were some hard words, too.
JENNY. I'm head cheerleader, in fact.
WALTER. I did good, too. I got a new important account. Everyone wanted it, but I got it.
ZOEY. I'm so proud of you, honey.
WALTER. And a raise. And a big promotion. Second one this week.
EILEEN. Your family is so amazing, Zoey.
JENNY. You're part of the family, too, Aunt Eileen.
ZOEY. That's right. I don't know how I'd get everything done around here without you.
WALTER. How about you, Zoey? What did you do today?
ZOEY. Is everyone done with their soup? Then I'll get the chicken and dumplings.
EILEEN. Let me do that, Zoey.

ZOEY stands.

ZOEY. No, you just sit there, Eileen. It's no trouble at all.

ZOEY gathers up everyone's soup bowl as she continues to talk.

ZOEY. I worked in the garden early, while it was still cool, and then I went and rode my horse for awhile—

As ZOEY talks, JENNY begins to tilt very slowly to one side, further and further, until she is in danger of falling off the side of her chair. It's a subtle motion, and no one seems to notice.

ZOEY. *(continuous)* —And I met some friends for coffee, and we went to the park, and petted the dogs…

Once ZOEY has gathered up all the bowls, she starts to exit R, but just before leaving the room, she turns around and returns to the table where she begins placing the very same bowls in front of each person, although not necessarily matching up each bowl with its previous owner.

ZOEY. *(continuous)* Okay, here we go, everyone—chicken and dumplings, with little baby peas mixed in, but no carrots.

WALTER/COBEY/JENNY/EILEEN. *(unison)* Eeewww, carrots.
COBEY. Cooked carrots are gross.

As ZOEY places a bowl in front of JENNY, ZOEY pushes her up straight once more into her seat.

ZOEY. You were about to fall on your punkin' head, Jenny.
JENNY. I hate cooked carrots. But I love peas.

ZOEY. Raw carrots are okay. Sometimes.

ZOEY takes her seat once more.

WALTER. I like raw carrots. If they're sweet. But not if they aren't.

ZOEY. We'll get a dog someday, I think.

AUNT EILEEN. We should. Dogs are nice, no matter what some people say.

WALTER. They don't always shed.

COBEY. They don't all have fleas. Not if you bathe them and brush them.

AUNT EILEEN. They don't always bark. Not if you give them toy bones and squeak toys to chew on.

JENNY. Can we? Can we please get a dog?

ZOEY. Maybe a Dalmatian. Like the ones in those old movies. With lots of spots.

WALTER. We could get a hundred and one of them. That would be fun.

ZOEY. No, not a hundred and one. Just one. Someday. …Someday, when… *(noticing that no one is eating)* Okay, everybody. Eat up! Eat while it's still hot.

On cue, everyone picks up their fork and starts miming eating from the empty bowls.

COBEY. Mmmm!

AUNT EILEEN. Delicious!

JENNY. The dumplings are my favorite.

AUNT EILEEN. So light and fluffy. No one makes dumplings like you, Zoey. The chicken is wonderful, too, of course.

ZOEY. Save room for dessert, though. There's ice cream. There's ice cream, and there's cinnamon apple pie.

MARGARET. *(off left; calling)* Zoey?

Instantly, everyone except ZOEY drops their hands into their laps and lowers their heads. Upon completing this action, they do not move. ZOEY looks off left in the direction from which MARGARET is calling. For a flicker of a second, she seems distracted, but she chooses to ignore the summons and takes another forkful from the empty bowl in front of her.

ZOEY. The ice cream is vanilla. But also mint chocolate chip, if you like that better.
MARGARET. *(off, but closer now; calling)* Zoey! What are you doing?
ZOEY. *(now in a slightly hushed tone and speaking more rapidly)* You can have both kinds if you want. Hurry up, now. Finish your dinners. If you don't finish, then you can't have any—
MARGARET. *(just off)* —Answer me! I know you can hear me! Don't you pretend you can't!

The sound of a door rattling. ZOEY stands. She hastily gathers up the bowls and rushes off R.

MARGARET. *(off)* Why is this door locked? Open it this instant! You know what I've told you about locking the door. ZOEY!!! Now!!! Open it right now!

The rattling continues. ZOEY 2 enters right. She is 8 years old and wears a dress and hairstyle identical to ZOEY's. She crosses left, pausing midway to look at the others seated around the table. They remain motionless, still gazing down into their laps. She continues to cross, exiting left.

MARGARET. *(off)* I am losing my patience. Do you want me to kick this door in? Do you want me to go get your Uncle Bill?

The sound of a door slamming open.

MARGARET. *(off)* What have I told you about ignoring me when I speak to you?

MARGARET enters from left. A few steps into the room, she stops, surveying the scene in front of her. ZOEY 2 follows, stopping just a step or two behind her.

MARGARET. What is all this? Why do you have all of this stuff out?

Beat. MARGARET turns to face ZOEY 2.

MARGARET. Well?
ZOEY 2. I…
MARGARET. I told you to come up here and get ready for bed thirty minutes ago. *(sweeping an arm in the direction of the table)* Is this what you call obeying me?
ZOEY 2. I forgot.
MARGARET. You forgot? I send you up here, and less than one minute later, you've forgotten what I told you to do. *(beat)* Is that it? Is that what you're telling me? …Answer me! Don't just stand there like a little imbecile! When someone asks you a question, you answer them! Well? …Don't you?
ZOEY 2. I was playing.
MARGARET. Yes. I can see that. This room was all picked up this afternoon, and now look at it.

MARGARET grabs ZOEY 2 roughly by the arm and shoves her a few steps towards the table.

MARGARET. I say, "Zoey, I want you to go upstairs and put on your pajamas," and you think that means, "Zoey, I want you to come up here and drag all your stupid stuffed animals out of the closet and make a big mess," is that it? …IS THAT IT???

ZOEY 2. No…

MARGARET. No? You don't think that's what I meant?

ZOEY 2 shakes her head No.

MARGARET. You look at me when I'm talking to you! Don't you stare at the floor, I've told you that a thousand times before! You… LOOK… at… me… when I am speaking to you. It's common courtesy! I will teach you manners, by God, if it's the last thing either of us ever do!

ZOEY 2 raises her head to look at MARGARET.

MARGARET. That's better. …And you know what I think? You know what I think the problem is? You have too many toys, that's what. Maybe if I hadn't given you so many things, you wouldn't get distracted. You wouldn't forget when I tell you to do something. Do you think that might be it?

Beat. ZOEY 2 looks at MARGARET, but does not answer her.

MARGARET. If we didn't have guests, I'd have your Uncle Bill come up right now. I'd have him come up and take a look at all this. That would be something, wouldn't it? …Go put on your pajamas. Right now. Right this minute.

ZOEY 2 crosses slowly right. MARGARET watches her slow progress.

MARGARET. Oh, for Pete's sake! I don't have all night! Move!
ZOEY 2. *(her back to MARGARET)* He's not my uncle.
MARGARET. What was that?
ZOEY 2. You call him that, but that isn't who he is. He's just a guy. He's just somebody you like.

ZOEY 2 turns to look back at MARGARET, who is momentarily at a loss for words. Beat. An unpleasant smiles grows on MARGARET's face as ZOEY 2 faces forward and exits right.

MARGARET. *(calling after her)* No, you're right. He isn't your uncle. And he's someone I like a lot. A whole lot. So you'll want to keep that in mind, missy. He doesn't like your antics any more than I do. And you know what? I was going to make you put all this crap away before you go to bed.

MARGARET has crossed to the table. She deliberately jostles the chair in which WALTER is sitting, causing him to tumble to the floor. He falls as though he has no bones in his body.

MARGARET. But I've changed my mind. I want you to leave everything just as it is. I want your uncle… *(correcting herself)* …I want *Bill* to see all this. I want him to know just how well you obey when I tell you to do something. I want him to get a real good idea of just what he's in for. I imagine he'll have a few things to say. And some ideas about what we should do. *(beat; calling off right)* Are you changing into your night things? …Zoey?
ZOEY 2. *(off)* Yes.
MARGARET. When you're ready, I want you to turn off the light and get into bed, you hear me? You go straight to bed. Our guests will be leaving in half hour or so, and then I'm going to come up and check on you. Bill will come with me. And you'd better be fast asleep, is all I have to say. …Understand? …You understand me?

MARGARET waits for an answer, but none comes. She heaves a sigh of exasperation, turns on her heels, muttering, and exits left.

A few seconds pass.

The original adult ZOEY enters right. She stands just inside the room, surveying the table, then crosses to it. She sits in her chair. WALTER remains on the floor, but the others lift their faces. They do not meet her gaze.

ZOEY. No ice cream, I guess.

ZOEY studies AUNT EILEEN for a second.

ZOEY. You're so stupid. You can't do anything at all.

EILEEN does not react to this.

ZOEY rises from her chair to lean across the table, looking at COBEY. After a second, she slaps him hard across the face.

His face remains turned in the direction she slapped him.

ZOEY looks next at JENNY, who does not look at her.

ZOEY. And you…

Pause. She glares at JENNY. For a second, it appears she might slap her, as well. But then ZOEY merely settles back into her chair.

ZOEY. You're too ugly to be head cheerleader. You're too ugly to be a cheerleader at all, you big liar.

JENNY does not react. After a second or so, ZOEY folds her arms on the table in front of her and buries her face in them. She remains like that for a few seconds. It would seem that she's about to cry, but then, she abruptly raises her head. There is a look of defiance on her face.

ZOEY. I don't care.

She stands, looking down at the others.

ZOEY. They can do whatever they want. They can put you in the trash, or give you away to the poor kids. It doesn't matter to me.

She is about to turn away, but first she places a hand on EILEEN's head. She strokes EILEEN's hair gently for just a couple of seconds before crossing right and exiting without a look back.

END OF PLAY

Girls Most Likely

CHARACTERS

CELESTE and MARION (same age; 50s–up)

SET REQUIREMENTS

A park bench (or three folding chairs representing a park bench)

Lights up on two women, MARION and CELESTE, sitting side by side. They are watching something in the distance. MARION is somewhat more elegant in both demeanor and attire. CELESTE is less so, wearing clothing perhaps slightly too young and too revealing for her, and a touch too much makeup.

Both women gaze into the distance for several seconds before CELESTE speaks.

CELESTE. God, I hated you in high school.

MARION. I think I hated you the first time I saw you, back in grammar school. If not right then, soon after. I knew you were trouble.

CELESTE. You were such a priss. Your little pinafore and your shiny buckle shoes. Acting like you were better than everybody else.

MARION. You deliberately splashed me with mud. Threw that ball right in the middle of that puddle. Don't tell me that was by accident.

CELESTE. Never said it was.

MARION. You liar. That's exactly what you told Mrs. Porter.

CELESTE. I can't believe you're still harping about it all these years later. Who remembers crap like that? Not me.

MARION. Not surprising. You weren't the one who had to go home with caked-on mud on your shoes.

CELESTE snorts.

MARION looks at her.

MARION. What? What's that?

CELESTE. Little Miss Fucking Perfect, whose life has been such a Popsicle dream, that she has nothing more to complain about fifty years later than a little mud on her shoes.

MARION. You are *such* a piece of work.

CELESTE looks critically at MARION for a few seconds, then looks away.

CELESTE. You don't have to sit here, you know.

MARION. I was here first. You think I should move, just because you came and parked your fat... just because you chose to sit down next to me? I'm not intimidated by you, Celeste.

CELESTE smiles. MARION looks at her.

MARION. What?

CELESTE. The only people who say they aren't intimidated by something are the ones who are.

MARION. I can't believe this! Sixty years old, and you're still a bully. Still acting like a junior high-schooler.

CELESTE. Says the woman who brought up the mud puddle.

MARION. Although, I don't know why I should expect anything more from someone who dresses like... like an '80s streetwalker.

Beat. CELESTE is trying to decide if she should get pissed over this. She can't. She actually laughs.

CELESTE. You even insult people like a priss. "Streetwalker?" Say I dress like a *whore*. Or a prostitute, at least. *(snorts)* "Streetwalker?" *(fanning herself as if she's been highly insulted)* My delicate ears!

MARION. Oh, I'm sure you're well-acquainted with the proper vernacular for things like that.

Beat. CELESTE tries to look down discreetly at her attire.

CELESTE. And there's nothing wrong with the way I'm dressed, by the way. It's the park; it's not Covent-Fucking-Gardens. Who are you dressed to impress, anyway? The joggers and the nannies and the four-year-olds?

MARION. I'm at least dressed age-appropriately.

CELESTE. Yeah? For when? The Victorian Age?

MARION picks up her purse, which has been sitting to her side, and begins digging through it.

CELESTE. Which one is yours, by the way?

MARION. *(still occupied with looking in her bag)* What?

CELESTE. Which kid? I'm guessing at least one of these children belongs to you. A grandchild. What else would bring you out here?

MARION stops searching in her bag for a moment and looks around. Then she looks at CELESTE.

MARION. Why do you want to know? So you can say a few insulting things about him or her, too?

CELESTE. Wow. You really think I have so little class, don't you?

MARION shrugs.

CELESTE. So, I heard you married Ricky Stafford.

MARION. Richard.

CELESTE. Huh?

MARION. It's *Richard.* Richard Stafford.

CELESTE. Oh. Well, pardon me. You did all right for yourself. Not that there was ever any doubt.

MARION. And you? Who'd you marry?

CELESTE. Which time?

MARION stares at her. CELESTE laughs.

CELESTE. Oh, come on. You'd've been disappointed if I'd said anything else. Like everybody, you had to have figured I was destined for multiple husbands. And you'd be right. Only two, though. Plus a live-in, here and there.

MARION. Really.

CELESTE. No, not really. One live-in, is all. Funny. That's the one that took. The one who's still around. Fourteen years. That's longer than both of the marriages put together.

MARION. Then… why haven't you…?

CELESTE. I learned it's the "I do" that's the real kiss of death.

MARION. Is it, now?

CELESTE. It's been my experience, anyway. Something about that little piece of paper seems to turn halfway decent guys into total jerks. Of course, I run with a different class of people than you do, I'm sure.

MARION begins digging in her purse once more.

CELESTE. You ever go to any of the reunions?

MARION. No.

CELESTE. Me, either. Who needs it? Who needs to be reminded of how wonderful other people's lives are? How big the houses they live in are, how all their children are rocket scientists and doctors and presidents of big companies. *(laughs)* I heard I won an award at the first one, though. Most kids in ten years. *Finally,* an award. And I wasn't even there to pick it up. Oh, well.

MARION has produced a package of cigarettes and a lighter from her bag. She puts a cigarette between her lips.

CELESTE. Oh, come on, now. You're not going to do that.
MARION. *(removing the cigarette for a second)* Do what? This? *(she puts the cigarette back in her mouth)*
CELESTE. It's a public place.
MARION. It's outdoors. If you don't like it, then move.

MARION starts to light the cigarette.

CELESTE. I'm not going to move.
MARION. Then hold your breath for the next three minutes.

Just as MARION is about to touch the flame to the cigarette, CELESTE snatches it out of her mouth and throws it over her shoulder.

Stunned, MARION stares at CELESTE. A second passes, and then CELESTE also snatches the lighter from her hand and throws that over her shoulder, as well.

MARION. How dare you? You pick that up!
CELESTE. Not a chance, sweetheart.

MARION stands, but CELESTE pulls her back into her seat.

CELESTE. And you're not going to pick it up, either.
MARION. *(struggling)* You get your hands off of me!

MARION swings at CELESTE. They begin to swat ineffectively at each other.

CELESTE. There are people all around—children! You're not going to pollute the air around them.

MARION. They're twenty-five feet away!

CELESTE. They can still see you! Your own grandchild can see you!

MARION stops swinging. She lowers her hands. CELESTE lowers hers, as well. MARION faces forward.

CELESTE. Kids are very impressionable. You want them to start smoking because they see you doing it and so they think it's all right?

MARION. Who the hell are you, some kind of a Girl Scout?

This completely catches CELESTE by surprise. She stares back at MARION. After a second, she starts to laugh.

CELESTE. Yeah. Oh, yeah, I'm a Girl Scout. A regular fucking Girl Scout, remember?

MARION can't help but grin at this, too.

MARION. *(smiling)* You know, if you're going to get on your high horse about secondhand smoke, I would at least like to remind you that dropping f-bombs right and left isn't exactly model behavior, either.

CELESTE raises her palms in an expression of surrender.

CELESTE. Fine. Miss Priss.

MARION. Oh, and can you drop the name-calling, as well? I'm not so much of a fucking prude as all that.

CELESTE looks somewhat impressed at the use of the cuss word.

MARION takes a moment to adjust her hair and shirt after the struggle.

MARION. And which one—or ones—are yours, by the way?

MARION points in the direction of the unseen "children."

MARION. I assume several of them?
CELESTE. Only five. I left the other eleven back in the trailer park today. There's not enough shoes to go around, so they trade off.

MARION laughs. She digs in her purse once more and comes up with a package of gum. She takes a stick, unwraps it and pokes it into her mouth, then offers the pack to CELESTE who looks at it but doesn't take one.

MARION. *(still holding it out)* Unless you have a moral objection to chewing gum, as well? Unless you think it might undermine the moral fiber of the children? *(she gestures to the unseen children)*
CELESTE. *(shaking her head)* I'm diabetic. But thanks.
MARION. Oh. *(putting the gum back into her bag)* I'm sorry.

There's a momentary awkward pause. Then CELESTE gestures outward.

CELESTE. The little snot-nosed brat digging in the dirt. The one with the duck on her shirt. She's mine. My only one, actually. None of my others have kids. Or want to have any. Because I was such a fine example of parenting, apparently.
MARION. Oh. *(looking outward)* Well, she's pretty.
CELESTE. She is, isn't she? She's what gets me up in the mornings.
MARION. You get to babysit her quite a bit?
CELESTE. If by quite a bit, you mean every day, all day, then yes.

MARION looks at CELESTE.

CELESTE. Her mama and daddy got themselves killed in a car accident.

Beat.

MARION. I'm sorry.

CELESTE. *(nodding)* I certainly didn't expect, at this stage of my life, to be starting over again, raising a four-year-old. I'll be seventy-four when she graduates high school. Oh, and she *will* graduate, I can promise you that. *(beat)* You know how there are all those times in your life when you say to yourself, "If I just had the chance to go back and do something all over again, I'd do it different the next time?" Well, I guess that's what this is. It's a terrible price to pay, getting to do something over again at the expense of your very own son, but how else am I to look at it?

CELESTE and MARION both gaze outward.

CELESTE. I figure I made every possible mistake with all the others. This time, this little girl… well.

MARION nods. A few seconds pass.

MARION. None of them belong to me.

CELESTE looks at MARION.

CELESTE. You don't have grandchildren?

MARION. I do. I don't get to see them often. I suppose that's why I come here sometimes. To be reminded of what my own grandkids might be doing right now. *(glancing at CELESTE and then looking away again)* I'm told that I was a rather cold mother. And wife, for that matter. *(rueful laugh)* So maybe you weren't so far wrong, after all. "Miss Priss," that's me. Dear Richard—oh, what the hell: *Ricky*—departed for greener pastures some years ago. For someone who didn't dress so age-appropriately, for somebody who could laugh if she got mud splashed on her shoes.

MARION looks at CELESTE again.

MARION. Now, please don't take this the wrong way... I didn't like you when we were growing up, and I still don't like you now. But there were one or two moments along the way when I would catch sight of you in the cafeteria or after school in the parking lot. You were usually doing something obnoxious or vulgar, surrounded by your cronies, and you'd be laughing hysterically. I'd wonder, "What's so funny?" and once or twice... maybe just one time, for one half-second, there'd be just the slightest sense of...
CELESTE. ...envy?
MARION. *(dismissively)* Oh, hardly! *(beat)* Of wondering what that might feel like. To just... let go... like that.
CELESTE. But it passed.
MARION. *(nodding)* Quickly. If it was ever there at all. Believe me, I had no desire to be *anything* like that. Anything like you.
CELESTE. *(considers this)* Makes sense.

Beat. CELESTE stands.

CELESTE. I'm outta here. *(calling)* GeeGee! You gather up your pail and shovel, darlin'. It's time to go!

CELESTE takes a step or two, then turns back to MARION.

CELESTE. You know, if you ever hope to spend a little more time around the grandkids, you'd better quit the cigarettes. You reek of smoke.
MARION. Mind your own damn business.

CELESTE smiles and turns away. She exits. MARION continues to stare directly ahead.

Lights fade.

END OF PLAY

A Little Game

("A Little Game" received its premiere in May 2018 at
Leeds University in the United Kingdom as part of
Gi60, The International One-Minute Play Festival.)

CHARACTERS
HENRY (30s or so), dad
APRIL and CHRISSY, (8 or 9 or so), HENRY's daughters
GRANDMOTHER (50s or so), HENRY's mother

SET REQUIREMENTS
A couch and an easy chair (or simply a few chairs)

Lights up on a living room/den. HENRY sits in a chair reading a book. GRANDMOTHER sits off to one side in another chair, doing nothing in particular. APRIL and CHRISSY are sprawled on the floor, coloring in coloring books.

A moment passes.

APRIL. Daddy?
HENRY. Yes, pumpkin?
APRIL. If we all went on a ship, and the ship started to sink, and there was only time to save one of us, who would you pick: Chrissy or me?
HENRY. Well, now, that's a silly question. We're not going on a ship.
APRIL. But if we did.
HENRY. We're not.

APRIL. But if we did.

CHRISSY. You said we might go on a Disney cruise sometime.

APRIL. See? So what would happen then?

HENRY. *If* we were on a ship… And *if* it began to sink, which it *wouldn't*… it would happen so slowly that there would be time to save both of you.

APRIL. But, what if it was like the Titanic? We learned in school that the Titanic went down real fast. *(rather pleased expression)* Lots of people died.

HENRY. That happened a long time ago. It would be different today. If a ship were to begin sinking for some reason—which it won't—and it sank fast—which it wouldn't—they would send plenty of helicopters to make sure everyone who didn't make it into a lifeboat—which they would—would be rescued.

APRIL. *(considers this; slightly disappointed)* Oh.

CHRISSY. What if there was a really bad storm? What if there was a hurricane, and no helicopters could get there, and what if some of the lifeboats had holes in them, and so there weren't enough for everybody? Who would you save then?

APRIL. Yeah! Who then, Daddy?

HENRY. In this day and age, they can predict when hurricanes will occur, so there would be plenty of time for ships to get out of the way of—

GRANDMOTHER. —Oh, for pity's sake, Henry, just answer the question and be done with it. Which one of the girls would you save?

HENRY. Mother, just stay out of this. April, it was a silly question, and you're trying to trick me into picking just one of you, and I'm not going to play that game.

    Beat.

GRANDMOTHER. I'd pick the prettier one. I'd pick April.

HENRY. Mother! *Mom!* For God's sake!

GRANDMOTHER. Well, the girl was waiting for an answer. Just because you were too much of a weenie to give her one...

HENRY. That's enough! April is not prettier than Chrissy!

Beat.

GRANDMOTHER. Such a weenie. That's one of the reasons I'd pick David over you.

HENRY. You'd... You'd pick David? If there was some life-and-death situation that forced you to save just one of your children, you'd choose my brother over me?

GRANDMOTHER. Well... You must have always suspected. Don't you feel better, finally knowing for sure?

HENRY. No! I don't!

GRANDMOTHER. Oh. I thought you would.

HENRY. So... Does that mean you think he's better looking than I am?

GRANDMOTHER. Oh, now, Henry, stop it. I'm not going to get drawn into your little game.

CHRISSY. *(to APRIL)* Grandma's right. You are prettier.

APRIL. Yeah. But only a little.

The girls return to coloring in their coloring books. HENRY continues to look indignantly at GRANDMOTHER as the lights fade.

END OF PLAY

Dawn's Early Light

CHARACTERS

IDEAL, a pleasant, if slightly disturbed, young woman in her 20s
MATT, a young man in his 20s, in slightly over his head

SET REQUIREMENTS

A bed

IDEAL's bedroom. IDEAL and MATT are in bed. The blankets conceal them up to their necks. IDEAL faces away from MATT, eyes closed. MATT is on his back, sitting up slightly, gazing upward.

IDEAL stirs. MATT immediately feigns sleep.

IDEAL. This is nice.

IDEAL studies MATT.

IDEAL. Isn't this nice? ...Come on now, I know you're not asleep. *(poking his face)* Wakey, wakey.

MATT opens his eyes.

MATT. What time is it?
IDEAL. Early. Does it matter?
MATT. I need to report back to the base by eleven.
IDEAL. Listen to you. Well, it's nowhere near eleven.

IDEAL wriggles closer to MATT. She drapes one arm across his chest.

IDEAL. Let's cuddle.

She wriggles against him.

IDEAL. Put your arm around me.

MATT reluctantly slides his arm under her raised head. She lowers her head on his arm.

IDEAL. Pull me close.

MATT does so. She rests her cheek against his chest.

IDEAL. I can hear your heart. …Boom… ba-doom… Boom… ba-doom…
MATT. Look…
IDEAL. Boom… ba-doom…
MATT. I really need to get going.
IDEAL. Boom… ba-doom. *(increasing the pace)* Ba-doom. Ba-doom. *(even faster now)* Ba-doom, ba-doom, ba-doom. It's beating faster. You're lying.
MATT. No, seriously.
IDEAL. We can't have a relationship that's built on lies, Matthew.
MATT. This isn't a relationship. You know that, don't you?
IDEAL. It could be. If you give it a chance.
MATT. We just met. Just a few hours ago.
IDEAL. What drew you to me? Last night, in the bar. Why, out of everyone there, did you pick me?
MATT. I don't know.

IDEAL clutches his jaw in her free hand, turning his face to her.

IDEAL. Don't say that! Of course you know. I wasn't just… a random *thing!* I'm a living, breathing person. I have *attributes!* Now, think back. The lights, the music, the people. There I was, at a table by myself. Why did you walk past all those other women, to me?

IDEAL takes her hand away from MATT's jaw.

MATT. Honestly?
IDEAL. Of course, honestly. Didn't I say that?
MATT. You were alone. No boyfriend hovering. No gal-pals hanging around you.
IDEAL. And?
MATT. And… you looked nice.
IDEAL. And?
MATT. I could tell you were checking me out. When you thought I wasn't looking.
IDEAL. *(smiling)* I was not!
MATT. You were.
IDEAL. I wasn't!
MATT. Now who's not being honest?
IDEAL. And?
MATT. I can't think of anything else.
IDEAL. Are you sure?
MATT. Yeah.
IDEAL. No, I think there's something more.
MATT. Yeah, there was one more thing, come to think of it. This was the last night of my leave. Tomorrow, it's back to the base, and then overseas for another tour of duty. I wanted one last piece of stateside ass. I'd struck out with the really hot babes, so I was looking through the leftovers, the desperate chicks who weren't *too* bad-looking… there you were. Sitting there, hoping I'd come over… So I did.

IDEAL studies MATT solemnly.

IDEAL. And how'd that work out for you?

MATT. Not well.

> *IDEAL sits up, throwing back the bed covers. She's wearing her dress from the bar. MATT is in a t-shirt but still wearing his slacks. His hand—the one we haven't seen—is handcuffed to the bedpost. From beneath the blankets, IDEAL produces a handgun.*

IDEAL. I realize this seems awkward… now. But it'll be a great story to tell our children. We'll look back on this and laugh.

MATT. I will never laugh about this, I can promise you that.

IDEAL. You're disappointed. I understand.

MATT. *Disappointed?* That's what you think?

IDEAL. You were hoping for a piece of ass. And that didn't happen.

MATT. The desire for that passed a while ago. You slipped something in the drink you gave me, didn't you? That's how *this* happened.

IDEAL. I'm just old-fashioned. I can't help it; it's the way I was raised. I'm saving myself for marriage. I'm saving myself for *you.*

MATT. You're going to kill me, aren't you? And dispose of my body, like you did with all the others.

IDEAL. What "others?" There haven't been others.

MATT. You expect me to believe this is the first time you've done this?

IDEAL. Of course it's the first time. What kind of a girl do you think I am?

MATT. I don't think I want to answer that. Not while you're holding that gun.

IDEAL. It's not the first time I've gone out, that's true. But it never felt right, not until now. Until then, it was never *you.* I *was* checking you out. But it wasn't until you came over, it wasn't until I looked in your eyes… that I knew. You were the one.

MATT. I'm not the one.

IDEAL. You meet someone and you fall in love and that's that.

MATT. It's not that. This isn't love.

IDEAL. It is for me.

MATT. It doesn't happen like that. It doesn't happen that fast. And it needs to involve two people.

IDEAL gestures to them both, indicating they are two people.

MATT. I don't love you.

IDEAL. Yet.

MATT. Ever.

IDEAL. You say that now…

IDEAL gets up, crossing to the other side of the bed, pointing the gun at MATT. She picks up a key from the nightstand next to the bed.

IDEAL. The key was sitting here, right in plain sight. You could have used it.

IDEAL unlocks the handcuffs.

MATT. I didn't see it.

IDEAL. You could have freed yourself. But you didn't.

MATT gets out of bed, snatching the gun. He grabs his shirt.

MATT. I didn't know it was there.

IDEAL. That's love, Matthew. Whether you know it or not.

MATT tests the weight of the gun.

MATT. It isn't loaded.

IDEAL. Of course not. *(smiles)* Love.

MATT tosses the gun on the bed and exits. Sound of a door slamming.

IDEAL sits on the bed, continuing to smile.

IDEAL. He'll be back.

BLACKOUT

END OF PLAY

Letter to the Committee

("Letter to the Committee" had its premiere in June 2015 at Black Box Theatre in Colorado Springs, Colorado.)

CHARACTERS

GLENN (late 20s–up), the pastor of the church
DALE, SARAH, PETE, DIDI (30s–up),
members of the congregation and the selection committee

SET REQUIREMENTS

5 folding chairs on an otherwise empty stage

Lights up on a small utilitarian sort of room. Chairs of different types form a semicircle. Seated in them are a group of individuals, all dressed in casual, but stylish, clothing. They are DALE, SARAH, PETE, DIDI and GLENN. All hold sheets of paper or have them nearby, draped over the arms of their chairs or in their laps. At rise, DALE reads from his. DIDI takes notes on a pad.

DALE. So, we'll offer the Douglases probationary membership.
SARAH. Making it clear that we'll be observing them closely for the next six months.
DALE. You'll take care of informing them, Glenn?

GLENN nods.

DALE. Next, the Inchmans.

General shifting in chairs, exchanges of glances.

PETE. Too soon to tell. Don't you think?

SARAH. I disagree.

DALE. I'm with Sarah. I think we have all the information we need.

GLENN. That's good. I've had several conversations with Mrs. Inchman—Janice—already, and I think she's—

SARAH. —We'll extend our profound regrets.

DALE. I can't imagine they'd be happy here, in any event.

GLENN. Well, now, that's not the impression I've gotten. They seem genuinely interested—

SARAH. —No, I really think it was just convenience that drew them here. They live just ten blocks away.

DIDI. On Templeton Square?

SARAH. *(nodding)* Can you imagine?

DALE. Well, maybe they didn't know. They're from out of state and wouldn't have any idea.

SARAH. Who knows what their realtor told them?

PETE. They'll figure it out soon enough.

DALE. I've run into Bob Inchman at the rec center.

SARAH. What did you think?

DALE. *(considering this)* He seems nice enough.

PETE. But would he fit in? That's the question.

DALE. Hard to tell. Probably not.

SARAH. You see? And really, what's the point of accepting their application, when the odds are, in two or three months, they'll realize their mistake all on their own.

PETE. So we're really doing them a favor, in any event. Saving them time. And awkwardness.

SARAH. *(making a note)* I'll send them the standard letter, in that case.

GLENN. I could talk to them. That just seems a little more straightforward. Maybe I could even—

PETE. —That's never a good idea, Glenn. It doesn't look as official. It's too folksy.

DALE. Plus, we know how you are.

General amusement and giggles from all except GLENN and DIDI.

SARAH. You may give them the wrong impression. As if there's hope.

DALE. *(consulting his paper)* Well, that's the last of the applicants. Unless I've overlooked anybody?

General shaking of heads, exchanges of glances.

DALE. That takes us to the autumn coat and food drive program. Last weekend of September, as usual. Any objections to keeping it the same?

General murmurs of assent.

DALE. And committee chairs. Now, Mona Evans has volunteered to head up publicity.

The murmurs continue, taking a vaguely disapproving tone, apart from GLENN and DIDI.

PETE. She hasn't done it before.

DIDI. But she works at the public television station.

SARAH. As she is so fond of reminding us. Endlessly.

GLENN. And isn't her background in marketing?

PETE. Yes, but Harriet Spivey has done such a good job in the past. Wouldn't it be a slap in the face to offer the position to someone else?

GLENN. Well, maybe they could co-chair.

SARAH. Oh, I don't think Harriet would stand for *that*.

PETE. And we don't want to run the risk of offending her.

GLENN. We don't?

DALE. Harriet can be very spiteful. She might undermine the whole thing if her feelings are hurt.

GLENN. You mean, she would actually discourage others from contributing to an event? An event designed to help people who might otherwise go hungry this winter?

The others exchange glances.

DALE. Well, but why run the risk? She's always done a fine job. I see no reason to rock the boat now.

Sounds of general assent.

SARAH. *(gesturing to DIDI to write this down)* So, Harriet for chair of the publicity committee, then.

DALE. We'll need to put out a request for drivers and people to man the collection boxes.

GLENN. I can make an announcement at the next service. Oh, and why don't we pull in a bunch of kids from the youth group to help out?

PETE. Teenagers?

DALE. They get awfully rowdy, don't you think?

SARAH. And distracted.

DALE. And distract*ing.*

SARAH. We certainly wouldn't want any of them driving. I'd fear for my life.

GLENN. Well, I can take responsibility for them. See to it that they don't get too distracted or rowdy. But I think you're underestimating them. They've got a lot of enthusiasm, and it would be an excellent opportunity for them to get a look at the greater good.

PETE. Enthusiasm. Is *that* what you call it?

DALE. Well… Maybe if Glenn thinks he can control them…

PETE. Oh, we're probably borrowing trouble, anyhow. Most of them won't show up anyway.

SARAH. Is that about it? It's nearly four forty-five. Traffic is going to be just horrible in fifteen minutes.

DALE. *(consulting his paper)* That's most everything. There are a few other items, but we can tackle those next time.

People begin to gather up their things, in the act of preparing to leave. DIDI is the first to stand. She crosses left.

DIDI. I'll unplug the coffee.

DIDI exits.

DALE. Glenn, have you noticed how ratty the lawn is looking? And the flowerbeds? Are we still using that little Korean guy to do our gardening?

GLENN. He's Vietnamese, actually. But yes.

PETE. You know, I'd been meaning to bring that up, too. Everything is looking so withered and brown.

DIDI returns, holding an envelope. She studies the front of it, then opens it and extracts a folded sheet of paper. She peruses it over the next few lines.

GLENN. Well, the problem is the water restrictions we're under. When you can only water things twice a week, and it's been as hot as it's been lately—

PETE. —Or maybe it's just some old-fashioned laziness.

SARAH. Didi, what do you have there?

DIDI. *(holding up the envelope and letter)* This was taped to the outside of the door. It's addressed to the Committee.

PETE crosses to take it from her.

PETE. The Committee? Let me see that.

DALE. That's odd. I don't remember seeing anything taped on the door when we came in.

PETE. There wasn't. One of us would have noticed.

SARAH. What does it say?

PETE, perusing the note, has a worried frown on his face. He lowers the letter without saying anything. DALE takes it from him and reads it. His own expression changes to one of concern and fear.

DALE. This… This is unbelievable. It's… it's garbage.

The others cluster around reaching for it.

SARAH. Oh, my God… *gosh,* I mean.

SARAH turns away, hand pressed to her stomach. She moves wobbily, as if on the verge of losing her balance.

PETE. It's a joke. That's all. An ugly sort of practical joke.

GLENN takes the letter to peruse it.

GLENN. *(reading aloud)* "…Behind your closed doors, in your little sanctum sanctorum…"

SARAH. Please… don't…

GLENN. "…Where you plot with glee the demise of others…"

GLENN pauses to look up with a troubled expression at everyone else in the room.

DALE. It's filth, is what it is. Scandal-mongering…

GLENN goes back to reading.

GLENN. *(reading)* …Confident that your own black hearts, your own sultry deeds remain secret. But maybe not so secret as you might think…"

DALE. You can stop, Glenn. We all saw what it says.

GLENN. *(reading)* "Do you want me to tell the others where I saw you on Wednesday evening? Or where you were last weekend? Or where you touched the…"

GLENN's expression changes to one of horror and revulsion. He lowers the letter, staring at the floor.

SARAH. I'm… I'm going to be ill…

SARAH rushes from the room.

PETE. Anonymous, of course. The coward's way.

DALE. And lies, of course. All lies.

PETE. The bastard couldn't even come up with names. That tells you something.

Everyone looks at everyone else uneasily.

PETE. *(uncertainly)* …Doesn't it?

GLENN. Of course it does. I'll destroy it.

DIDI. Destroy it? What good will that do?

PETE. Didi…

DIDI. Whoever wrote it… he's still out there.

DALE. Oh, forget him. *(beat)* Or her.

Which causes all of them to look uneasily from face to face.

DALE. Whoever it is, is just fishing, just… just throwing random stuff out there maliciously. There's no proof. There's no proof, because none of that is true. We know that!

Uncertain silence.

PETE. I have to go…

PETE moves to the door.

DALE. Pete…? Didi…? Reverend…? You realize that, don't you? That this is just some sort of a nasty prank. We… we know each other. We've known each other for *years!*
PETE. But… but why? Why would somebody even do this?
DALE. I… I don't know. Do crazies even need a reason? They just… they like stirring things up, is all.

DALE crosses to GLENN and snatches the letter from him.

DALE. Give me that!

DALE looks at it for a second, then, in a fury, tears it into small pieces, scattering them everywhere.

DALE. That's what I think about all that!

DALE storms out. PETE follows.

DIDI watches them go, then turns to look at GLENN, who kneels to gather up all of the pieces of paper.

DIDI. What… What's going to happen, do you think?
GLENN. I don't know, Didi.
DIDI. Do you think it's true? Any of what was in there?
GLENN. I… I don't think it matters any more.

GLENN stands and looks at DIDI. She has a searching look on her face.

DIDI. Are you going to tell me that the Lord moves in mysterious ways?

GLENN. I wouldn't presume to lecture. Certainly not now.

GLENN turns away, then turns back to look at her curiously.

GLENN. No one has been in the building all afternoon, Didi. Except for the members of the Committee.

GLENN looks down at the pieces of paper in his hands.

GLENN. And you're the only one who left the room once we were all here.

Just the slightest hint of a smile crosses his face. A second later a similar almost-smile crosses DIDI's, as well.

DIDI. He does, you know. *(beat)* He moves that way. Some of them more mysterious than others.

DIDI looks at GLENN a second longer, then turns and crosses, exiting the room.

GLENN looks again at the pieces of paper he's holding, then back up in the direction of DIDI's exit.

The lights fade.

END OF PLAY

With Raspberry Jelly in the Middle

*("With Raspberry Jelly in the Middle" had its premiere February 2017
at the Napa Valley Short Play Festival in Napa, California.)*

PLAYWRIGHT'S NOTE: While sometimes it works to have an adult actor play a child simply by dressing them accordingly and having them behave in childlike fashion, I strongly discourage that in this case. Even though it can be problematic to find a young girl capable of playing a role like that of BELINDA, casting an older actress in the role would lend this play a decidedly "kinky" feeling, which was definitely not my intention.

CHARACTERS

BELINDA, a 7-year-old girl
WALTER (40s–up), a friend of her parents

SET REQUIREMENTS

A child's card table and four chairs situated around it

At rise, BELINDA, in a frilly spring dress, sits at a child's card table, humming and talking to a collection of dolls and stuffed animals. She pours imaginary tea from a plastic teapot into a collection of plastic cups and saucers situated in front of the dolls and stuffed animals sitting in the other three chairs. A stuffed bear sits in the chair directly opposite BELINDA.

BELINDA. And that's for *you*... And here's some for *you*... And also some for you.

BELINDA sets the teapot in the middle of the table and picks up a small plastic pitcher.

BELINDA. And who would care for cream? ...Yes, please... No thank you... Just a smidge...

She speaks in turn as she offers the pitcher around the table. She sets down the plastic pitcher and takes up a plastic sugar bowl.

BELINDA. One lump or two? *(addressing the stuffed bear)* Oh, I know that you like three, Monty... *(to the others)* And one for you... And two for you... I'm sorry I have to use my fingers, but I've lost the tongs, and Mommy's are too big to fit into this bowl—

WALTER, a distinguished, slightly portly looking gentleman in a suit and tie, appears in the doorway. He pauses, watching all of this with amusement.

BELINDA. —and as a special treat, there are cookies, too. I made them myself, just this morning.

BELINDA sets down the plastic sugar bowl and takes up an empty plastic plate.

BELINDA. They are hot chocolate marshmallow strawberry short-cake cookies. Careful... they're still hot.

WALTER steps into the room.

WALTER. Ooh, hot chocolate marshmallow strawberry shortcake cookies… my favorite! May I have one?

BELINDA is startled by his entrance. She freezes and stares up at him with misgiving.

WALTER. I heard there was a much better party going on up here than the one downstairs. They don't have anything as nice down there. Mostly just brandy and cigar smoke. Do you drink brandy and smoke cigars?

BELINDA stares at him without answering.

WALTER. …Oh, am I intruding?
BELINDA. This is a tea party.
WALTER. Yes, I see.
BELINDA. For little girls. Little girls don't smoke cigars or drink brandy.
WALTER. No, of course not. How silly of me.

WALTER lifts the stuffed bear from the chair on the opposite side of the table from BELINDA.

WALTER. Would your bear object to my sharing his seat?
BELINDA. His name's Monty.
WALTER. *(addressing the bear)* Hello, Monty. Would you mind if I joined the party? Just long enough for half a cup of tea and a cookie? *(holding the bear's face to his ear, as if listening)* …He says it would be all right, as long as it's just half a cup, and just one cookie. *(beat)* And if it's okay with his hostess.

BELINDA continues to regard WALTER warily.

WALTER. That's you.
BELINDA. I know what a hostess is. *(after a final few seconds of debate)*

All right.

WALTER pulls out the small chair and situates himself somewhat uncomfortably on it. His knees are nearly up to his chin. He positions the stuffed bear carefully in his lap.

WALTER. Well, thank you, that's very kind. And Monty will sit here, in my lap.
BELINDA. You'll have to share his cup. I only have four.
WALTER. I don't mind, if Monty doesn't.

BELINDA picks up each cup and dumps the pretend tea back into the teapot.

BELINDA. We'll start again. The tea has gotten cold.

BELINDA repositions all the cups and saucers and begins pouring a round of tea. She hums self-consciously, occasionally glancing at WALTER.

WALTER. This looks very tasty. Is it Darjeeling?
BELINDA. Huh?
WALTER. That's a very fine tea that comes all the way from India.
BELINDA. I don't know.

WALTER lifts the cup to his lips and takes a sip.

WALTER. Oh, yes. Very delicious. That's Darjeeling, all right.
BELINDA. *(almost accusingly)* You didn't wait for me to ask if you wanted cream or sugar.
WALTER. Oh, I'm sorry. I was just so thirsty, you see.
BELINDA. You don't know how to play this.
WALTER. Well… the tea was excellent as it was. I don't think I would

have taken sugar or cream anyway.

BELINDA hands cream and sugar around to the others.

BELINDA. *(as she does this)* That's not the point. You're supposed to wait until I ask.
WALTER. *(contritely)* Of course. I'll remember from now on.

BELINDA finishes serving cream and sugar. She picks up the plate.

BELINDA. Now: Who would like a cookie? They're butterscotch coconut raisin with… with raspberry jelly in the middle!
WALTER. Oh… I thought they were hot chocolate marshmallow strawberry shortcake.
BELINDA. *(impatiently)* That was before. These are new cookies.

WALTER starts to reach for an imaginary cookie. BELINDA moves the plate away.

BELINDA. You have to wait your turn!
WALTER. *(amused)* Of course.

BELINDA offers the plate to the chair on her left.

BELINDA. Would you care for a cookie? *(pause)* All right.

BELINDA sets a cookie in front of the doll or stuffed animal in that chair. Then she directs the plate to WALTER and the stuffed bear.

BELINDA. Would you care for a cookie?
WALTER. Well… I *was* hoping for a hot chocolate marshmallow one… but okay. Thank you very much.

WALTER takes a "cookie" and pops it into his mouth, pretending to chew.

BELINDA stares at him coldly. WALTER senses he has displeased her in some way, and to compensate, he holds up the bear.

WALTER. How about you, Monty? Would you care for a cookie?

BELINDA snatches the plate away.

BELINDA. No. He doesn't want one. He doesn't like this kind.

BELINDA extends the plate to the chair on her right.

BELINDA. *(to the occupant of that chair)* Would you like one?

She listens, then sets a pretend cookie in front of that doll or stuffed animal. She sets the plate in the center of the table, and picks up her teacup and takes a sip.

WALTER. How about the hostess? Doesn't she want a cookie?

BELINDA. *(addressing the occupant in the chair to her left)* And how have you been lately? How are your children? *(listening)* Uh-huh. Uh-huh.

WALTER lifts the plastic teacup to the stuffed bear's face.

WALTER. Allow me to serve you, sir.

BELINDA. *(to the chair on her left)* What's that? You're not feeling well? Oh, dear.

BELINDA abruptly swings her arm, striking the doll or stuffed animal in the chair to her left, sending it hurtling across the room.

BELINDA. You're dead now.

WALTER, stunned, freezes, watching this. BELINDA turns to the chair on her right. She picks up the occupant of that chair, holds it overhead, and then dashes it cruelly to the ground.

BELINDA. You're dead, too. Poisoned! Stupid, stupid doll!

BELINDA glares angrily at the doll on the ground. After another second or two, she composes herself and smiles sweetly across the table at the stuffed bear in WALTER's lap.

BELINDA. But not you, Monty. You're not dead. You guessed right.
WALTER. *(flustered)* That... That wasn't a very nice thing to do, Belinda. Treating your friends—your playthings—like that.
BELINDA. They were stupid. They lost the game. Monty's the only one who won.
WALTER. Won? What's the game?
BELINDA. At every tea, one thing is poisoned. But only I know what it is. Last time, it was the sugar. This time, it was the butterscotch coconut raisin cookies with the raspberry jelly. The jelly is the poisoned part. And so now, all the ones who ate it are *dead!*

BELINDA leers at WALTER in a most unsettling way.

WALTER. That's... That's an awful game, don't you think? Is that the kind of thing little girls should be playing?

BELINDA continues to stare steadily at WALTER. He begins to blink and his face begins to contort.

BELINDA. *You* ate the cookie.

WALTER. Belinda… Can you go and get your Mommy or your Daddy?

BELINDA. You should have said No, thank you, I don't care for one.

WALTER. *(clutching at his throat)* Uncle Walter isn't feeling very well.

BELINDA. If you'd been here sooner, if you'd had one of the hot choco-late marshmallow strawberry shortcake cookies, you would have been fine. *Those* weren't poisoned.

BELINDA stands and reaches across the table to take the stuffed bear from his hands.

WALTER. Belinda… sweetheart… please go get somebody…

WALTER attempts to stand, but instead topples out of the small chair onto the ground. He begins spasming and writhing. BELINDA watches this impassively.

BELINDA. Monty is nearly always the smart one. He almost never dies.

BELINDA turns the bear to face her and she hugs him to her chest, closing her eyes and cuddling him fondly.

WALTER continues to writhe and twitch.

BELINDA opens her eyes and looks around the room.

BELINDA. Okay, who should we get to play the game this time?

BELINDA moves around the table and steps carefully over WAL-TER's still-twitching form, paying him no attention whatsoever. She crosses to a toy chest and lifts the lid. She extracts three more stuffed animals or dolls.

BELINDA. *(addressing the toys)* Do *you* want to play this time? And you? You didn't do very well last time, but all right. Maybe you'll guess better today.

WALTER now lies still, breathing faintly. BELINDA steps back across him and positions the new toys in their chairs, then takes her seat. WALTER feebly raises his hand in her direction.

WALTER. *(faintly)* Belinda..?

BELINDA pours the imaginary tea out of the tea cups back into the pot.

BELINDA. I can't hear you. You're dead.

WALTER's hand drops to the floor. BELINDA begins to hum again as she refills the tea cups.

The lights fade as the game proceeds.

END OF PLAY

The Disposable Emotion

A fictional conversation between
Queen Elizabeth I and Mary, Queen of Scots

PLAYWRIGHT'S NOTE: I'm fascinated by the long and bloody history of the English monarchy, and the fact that so much blood was shed, frequently at the direction of one member of the Royal Family against another. The mere fact of being born into royal lineage immediately set you up as a potential murder victim to prevent your ascension to the throne by a more ambitious relative who had his—or her—sights on the position.

In this piece, I tried to imagine what form a conversation between two such family members might take, where ambition trumps familial love. I doubt the two women spent any time together as children, but certainly there were members of the monarchy who did—and who later plotted the demise of someone who had once been a beloved companion.

CHARACTERS
ELIZABETH and MARY, both in their 30s

SET REQUIREMENTS
Two stools set some distance apart

Lights up on two stools positioned on an otherwise empty stage. ELIZABETH sits on the stage-right stool. A shadow cast on the curtain behind her suggests a crown or scepter. MARY sits on the stage-left stool. A shadow cast on the curtain behind her suggests the verti-

cal bars of a cell. Both women wear black long-sleeved shirts, black slacks and black shoes. During their exchanges, they never look at one another, but only directly out toward the audience.

ELIZABETH. One of my earliest memories is of you, swaddled and in your crib. I was four, and spellbound. You were the most beautiful thing I had ever seen. Large blue eyes, golden hair, much fairer than it is now. I reached down and your fingers wrapped around just one of mine and squeezed it so softly. And I thought, "I love you, and it makes me sad to know I will kill you one day."

MARY. As soon as I could walk, I began tottering around after you. You moved with such grace, or so it seemed to me, and without effort. There were our parents and the nurses, of course, but no one mattered as much to me as you did. Perhaps because you were nearer to my own size.

ELIZABETH. There was Edward, of course, but he died. And that made all the difference. It wouldn't have had to be this way if he had just tried harder to live.

MARY. Or if there'd been other boys.

ELIZABETH. *(nodding)* How unfair it all is, the sexism and the birth order. Harder on the males, I suppose, since they are never out of it. The females can escape it if the circumstances are right, if there are enough brothers. Especially brothers who live to have sons. The arrival of every new male makes the female breathe just a little more easily. Unless she is ambitious.

MARY. You're ambitious, Lizzie.

ELIZABETH. Because I was afraid you were, Mary. Or would become so.

MARY. Fair enough.

ELIZABETH. One of the nurses had said to me, before I ever saw you, but after you were born, "Well, you'll have to be careful now, child. You'll want to sleep with one eye open, going forward."

MARY. So I have Nurse to thank for my current predicament.

ELIZABETH. In a manner of speaking.

MARY. It's a curious thing to have your destiny mapped out for you before you have even arrived. To be born already condemned to die because, even before you can see or hear or crawl, you pose a threat. And not to just anyone, but to the person closest to you.

ELIZABETH. So dramatic. After all, the very act of being born condemns all of us to die, doesn't it?

MARY. I'll use that thought to console me in my last moments.

ELIZABETH. I don't hate you, Mary. I never have, not for a minute. And I really only began to fear you when you were ten or twelve. That's when I worried that you'd begun to have ideas. After all, I had to assume Nurse was whispering in your ear, as well.

MARY. Nobody bothered to whisper to me. They whispered about me, was all. I used to wonder what was wrong, what all that whispering and glancing and nudging one another could mean. Even Mother looked at me oddly. I used to think she just didn't love me as much as she loved you. Now I understand she realized that loving me very much at all was just a wasted emotion.

ELIZABETH. So you were jealous.

MARY. Of some things, yes. But not that, Lizzie. Not of your position. I would happily have gone to another corner of the world where I could have forgotten all that and been forgotten. I tried.

ELIZABETH. I know. I know you did.

MARY. Even now I am far away. I would be content to remain like this.

ELIZABETH. But I would not be content to *have* you remain like that.

MARY. I am not in a position to do you harm in any way.

ELIZABETH. You are always in the position. So long as you draw breath, you are a temptation for any malcontent or traitor who might like to use you as a pawn, to represent an agenda more to their own liking.

MARY. People will wonder why you do this.

ELIZABETH. Let them wonder.

Several seconds pass.

ELIZABETH. No further questions? No more pleas?

MARY. None.

ELIZABETH. Do you hate me, then?

MARY. Would that give you better justification for what you are going to do?

ELIZABETH. I don't know. It might.

MARY. Just as Mother saw no point in loving me, it seems that hating you would be a wasted emotion now.

ELIZABETH. Very wise.

MARY. I will entertain your brother Edward with stories until the two of you can be reunited.

ELIZABETH. You do that, Mary. And pleasant dreams.

MARY. You as well, dear cousin.

The women stare forward as the lights slowly fade to black.

END OF PLAY

Café Coeur Brisé

(Written as part of the Mile High 24 Challenge, "Café Coeur Brisé" was first performed at The Edge Theater, Lakewood, Colorado, in June 2016.)

CHARACTERS
Stephen 20s/30s, waiter
Lowell 30s/40s, customer
Yvonne, 20s/30s, customer
Jarrod, 20s/30s, customer

SET REQUIREMENTS
3 mismatched tables, each with 2 mismatched chairs

Lights up on a small "hole-in-the-wall" café, which has definitely seen better days. Three small mismatched tables decorate the space, each with a couple of mismatched chairs.

At rise, LOWELL sits at one table reading a newspaper. YVONNE sits at another, reading a hardcover book. The book does not have a dust jacket and appears to be somewhat old and battered. On one of the chairs at the empty table rests a Chinese hat.

STEPHEN stands off to one side, slouching. He wears a waiter's apron or smock. He's doing nothing in particular, just passing time and generally ignoring customers. Occasionally he inspects his fingers and bites a hangnail.

JARROD enters right. He pauses, looking around the café.

STEPHEN. *(gesturing, but not moving from where he is standing)* Sit anywhere.
JARROD. Um… Okay.

Beat. Clearly there is only one table that isn't occupied. JARROD crosses and sits at that one. He's a little nervous, rubbing his hands on his pants legs.

A few seconds pass. He clears his throat. This causes YVONNE to look at him. He smiles at her. She does not smile back. She turns a page and goes back to her reading.

JARROD takes a folded piece of paper from his pocket, unfolds and studies it, then puts it away again.

LOWELL has also noticed the newcomer.

LOWELL. Waiting for someone?
JARROD. Me?
LOWELL. You.
JARROD. Uh, yeah.
STEPHEN. Coffee?
JARROD. What?

JARROD looks toward STEPHEN, who does not repeat the question.

YVONNE. He wants to know if you want coffee.
JARROD. Oh. *(to STEPHEN)* Not right now. Maybe later.

STEPHEN shrugs. JARROD looks around the place.

JARROD. I had a terrible time trying to find this place. I was afraid I was going to be late. *(looking at YVONNE)* You… You aren't by chance Rose, are you?

YVONNE. Do I look like a Rose?

JARROD. …No. Not actually.

YVONNE. *(lowering her book)* What's *that* supposed to mean?

JARROD. Nothing. I didn't mean anything. I just… I'm waiting for a Rose.

Snorts of laughter from LOWELL, STEPHEN and YVONNE. JAR-ROD is a little bewildered by that.

JARROD. That's her name. We're supposed to be meeting here.

LOWELL. Ah. A date.

YVONNE. A blind date.

JARROD. Yeah. She… She said I'd know her because she'd be reading a book.

YVONNE sets down the book.

YVONNE. Oh, well, then, I must be your girl.

JARROD. I'm sorry. I just thought… Never mind. So… nobody else has been here in the last few minutes? Someone who looked like they might be looking for somebody?

STEPHEN shakes his head No.

JARROD. Oh. Well, I'm early. Almost.

LOWELL. *(to YVONNE)* What is that you're reading, anyway? You always seem to have it with you. Must be very interesting.

YVONNE. Oh, it's fascinating. It's called *None of Your Damn Business.*

YVONNE picks up the book again and resumes reading. STEPHEN approaches her table, leaning down to look at the cover.

STEPHEN. *The Razor's Edge.* By Somerset... Somerset MAG...HAM.
YVONNE. It's pronounced *MOM*. Somerset Maugham. Jeez. Get an education, why don't you?
LOWELL. Fascinating story. Rather depressing, though.
YVONNE. That depends upon your point of view. And I happen to *like* depressing. It suits me.
STEPHEN. What's it about?

LOWELL stands and crosses down to YVONNE's table.

LOWELL. It's about an American expatriate living in Paris, a war veteran who can no longer bring himself to believe in anything. Two women are in love with him. One falls into an unhappy marriage with someone else, and the other one dies.
STEPHEN. Wow. Barrel of laughs.
YVONNE. It's a true account of romance, is all.
LOWELL. So cynical. Someone must have hurt you pretty badly.
YVONNE. I'm fine. Just let me read my book in peace.
JARROD. I believe in romance.

The others look at him.

JARROD. Whether anyone shows up here tonight, or not.
LOWELL. Good for you.
YVONNE. Let's see if you still feel that way when you're sitting there alone in another hour.

STEPHEN crosses back to where he stood originally. LOWELL goes back and sits at his table. He studies his paper for a few seconds, then looks up at YVONNE.

LOWELL. I'd say you have a sentimental attachment to that book. Reading it over and over again.

YVONNE ignores him.

LOWELL. You know what I think? …I think you're a romantic, same as our friend over here. *(gesturing to JARROD)* I'd venture to say you've wept a time or two as you've read it. Probably at the same passages each time… And why not? It's a very compelling, very moving story. We want a happy outcome. And when we don't get it, well…

STEPHEN. I like *horror* novels. Stephen King. Stuff like that. …Well, not novels. But horror movies. Who has time to read?

JARROD has just discovered the Chinese hat sitting on the other chair at his table. He has picked it up and is examining it.

JARROD. Whose is this?

STEPHEN. It's been there all day. Maybe all week. Somebody left it. I don't know who. If it's still there tomorrow, maybe I'll put it in the lost and found. …Or I'll start a lost and found.

JARROD. *(pointing to the symbol on the hat)* I wonder what this means.

YVONNE. Maybe Rose left it for you. Maybe it means "sorry."

JARROD. Maybe it means "hope." Or "beauty."

YVONNE. Maybe it means "dry clean only."

LOWELL has risen and moved down to look over JARROD's shoulder during all of this. He takes the hat from JARROD.

LOWELL. It means "warrior," actually.

STEPHEN. Really? How do you know that?

LOWELL. You pick up things, here and there, as you go along.

LOWELL sets the hat on JARROD's head.

YVONNE. I knew it didn't mean "beauty." *(to LOWELL)* And for your information, yes. I do believe in romance. I'm just realistic about it.

LOWELL. I'm glad to hear that. I think.

YVONNE. What I don't believe in, is happily ever after.

STEPHEN. You mean, like in fairy tales?

YVONNE. Exactly. *(to JARROD)* Take that thing off. You look ridiculous. Plus, you don't know where it's been.

JARROD removes the hat.

LOWELL. There's a case to be made for that. The no-happily-ever-afters, I mean.

STEPHEN. My dad's been married four times. He's had a lot of happily ever afters.

LOWELL. That illustrates my point, young man. Sort of. Romantic stories and movies have done us a disservice. They conclude at the point where the hero and heroine have resolved their differences, overcome tremendous odds, and now they've settled down to a future of unlimited bliss together.

JARROD. But isn't that what we all want?

LOWELL. It's what we *think* we want. Until we get it. Fortunately, not many of us do. Do you understand how boring, how *unchallenging* eternal bliss would be?

LOWELL takes the Chinese hat and drops it back on the chair where JARROD found it.

LOWELL. We're all warriors, after a fact, when it comes to love and romance.

STEPHEN. I don't understand.

LOWELL. The yearning. The frustration. The petty arguments. And the big ones. The blind dates who don't show up. *(hastily correcting himself for JARROD's sake)* Or who are late. *Those* are the things that keep life interesting. What's a good romance without a dragon or two to slay along the way? And if it can't be dragons, then it should be ridiculous misunderstandings, and fights about working too late, and crying babies, and dogs upchucking on the carpet.

STEPHEN. So nobody should fall in love, ever?

LOWELL. Of course they should. It's a wonderful, terrific leap of faith, with sharp, scary boulders far below, just waiting to break every bone in our body when we fall. How do we know it's even happened, if we don't have a few bumps and bruises to show for our efforts?

STEPHEN. *(considering this for a second)* You're one weird dude.

YVONNE. I have to agree with him there.

LOWELL. You keep coming back to that same book, again and again. Because it doesn't end the way you want it to. Maybe each time you read it, you hope that, this time, things will turn out better.

YVONNE. No. I don't think that.

JARROD. Pursuit.

The others look at him.

YVONNE. What?

JARROD. Pursuit. The thrill of the chase. And when, after all that, you find the person who loves you back, you want things to stay that exciting always. You don't want to ride off into the sunset. Well, sure, you want sunny skies some of the time. But only if there's the occasional thunderstorm, too.

LOWELL. *(pleased)* My work here is done.

LOWELL crosses back up and sits at his table, picking up his newspaper.

YVONNE. You are *both* cray-cray. And I need to use the bathroom.

YVONNE stands. As she crosses to exit left, she addresses STEPHEN.

YVONNE. Maybe there could be a glass of wine sitting on my table when I get back? If I'm not taking you away from any other important duties?

STEPHEN. Red or white?

YVONNE. Surprise me. *(she starts to leave, then turns back)* No. Make it white. Chablis.

YVONNE exits left.

STEPHEN. *(to JARROD)* You decided if you want coffee?

JARROD is reaching into his pocket. He extracts his phone and studies the screen. He is reading a text in silence. Both STEPHEN and LOWELL watch him. After a few seconds, he puts his phone back in his pocket.

JARROD. No. Nothing, thanks.

STEPHEN exits left. A few seconds pass.

JARROD. She isn't coming.

LOWELL. I'm sorry. …Did she say why?

JARROD shakes his head. He stands.

LOWELL. Well, look… Can I buy you a glass of wine or something? A beer?

JARROD. No. Thanks.

JARROD turns to exit right, then, after a second, turns back.

JARROD. Sometimes it's a little harder to keep believing than other times. I understand all that about being a warrior. But sometimes…

Sometimes, you just want somebody to show up. *(gesturing to YVONNE's table)* At least she wasn't here to see this.

As LOWELL watches, JARROD crosses slowly right. Just as he is about to exit, LOWELL speaks.

LOWELL. Good night.

JARROD does not look back, but he raises his hand in a defeated sort of wave. He exits.

LOWELL heaves a big sigh.

STEPHEN enters left, carrying YVONNE's wine. He sets the glass on her table.

STEPHEN. *(gesturing to JARROD's empty table)* He's gone?
LOWELL. He is.
STEPHEN. She didn't show?
LOWELL. She did not.
STEPHEN. Poor bastard.
LOWELL. Not really.

STEPHEN picks up the book YVONNE has been reading. He opens the front cover.

STEPHEN. Huh.
LOWELL. What?
STEPHEN. *(reading an inscription on the first page)* Look at this… "If lost… please return to Yvonne Rose Carter."

STEPHEN looks at LOWELL.

STEPHEN. You don't think…? Are you telling me…?

LOWELL smiles.

LOWELL. Warriors. I don't think the story's over yet.

END OF PLAY

Act Two
MONOLOGUES

Monologue from

Ignoring the Emptiness

THERESA
Late 40s to 60s

My husband left the other day.

Not on a trip. Well, maybe on a trip. I don't really know. But he *left* left. As in not coming back "left." Technically, I'm married. But it doesn't feel like it.

On Monday morning, I was in the kitchen, slicing up a banana for corn flakes, and he walked in with his suitcase. He said, "Well, I guess this is it." I looked at him and said, "*What's* it?" He gestured around the room and said, "All this. Us. But I want you to know I've really enjoyed myself the past thirty years." And I said, "Oh. All right." And then he left. Closed the door and was gone.

For one strange moment, I stood there thinking, "Maybe he didn't *want* banana on his corn flakes all this time. Was that it?" But of course, I knew it wasn't really that.

I wanted to be hurt. I wanted to feel angry. I finished slicing the banana and then I sat down and had breakfast, all the while waiting to feel something. But I didn't. The whole thing seemed to have reached its logical conclusion. The mortgage is paid, the kids are raised. Wasn't that everything we were supposed to do?

All the rest of our days, waking up and looking at each other without any other distractions. I don't think he could face that. It's as if he realized it five minutes before I did... My husband and I... Oh, I guess I should stop saying it like that... My ex-husband and I, we were just so casual about everything. We wandered into the marriage, and now we've wandered back out again.

At the Far End of the Garden

BEN
30s–up

One time, a few years back, I left here later than usual one night. Don't remember what held me up. It was a nice evening. Warm. I decided to walk a different way. I was looking up at the stars, so I don't know when I first realized there was a fellow walking alongside me. Well, not with me. A step or two behind. Gave me a start. I was a little pissed, if you want to know the facts, but then I figure it's probably some drunk from the bar up the road, tottering on home, or lost or something. I can smell the booze on his breath. We walk a little ways, and he still doesn't say anything. I slow down, he slows down. I speed up, he speeds up. I stop. He doesn't pass me. Now I'm thinking my head's about to get bashed in for beer money or something. So I decide I'm at least going to be looking at him when he tries, and I start to turn. "Don't," he says. "Don't look. You don't want to see."

But I did. I clench my fists, and I turn. There's nobody there. Not a soul. Just me, and the night, and the stars. So whose voice did I hear? Whose breath was I smelling? A little further on, I see some flashing lights down at the junction. When I get close, I can tell it's a sheriff's car and a fire truck and an ambulance. A mangled car, too, crunched up against the power pole. "Some drunk," the ambulance driver tells me. He's leaning against the side of the fire truck, because he ain't in a hurry no more. I was still standing there when they pulled the body out from behind the wheel. Wish I hadn't been. Wish I hadn't looked. Hadn't seen what a pole and a busted windshield can do to a face.

You ask me what I think? I think I oughta go back to walking home the old way. That's what I think.

Your Dilly Dilly Heart

DANIELLE
Late 20s to late 30s

I was seventeen and starting my senior year when I first laid eyes on him. Rockaway wasn't exactly a small town, but it wasn't so big that you didn't know practically everybody in school. There were three new kids that fall. Tim and Roselle Chambers, brother and sister. And there was Beau Saint Every, the mystery kid. Staying with Sam and Paulette Hendry. He wasn't their son. They didn't have kids. Yet all of a sudden, there he was, living at their place.

Beau Saint Every swaggered into English Lit that morning, and everybody looked up, including Mrs. Ontmeyer. You know, now that I look back, he wasn't much besides a scrawny little dweeb in black jeans and a kind of polo shirt that must have come from the Salvation Army thrift store or someplace, because it hung practically down to his knees. But he sold it, you know? Had the attitude down completely. Not just that he didn't want to be there; more that you knew he'd already made up his mind he wasn't going to learn anything in that class. Up until then, I'd kind of been thinking I'd hook up with that other new kid, Tim Chambers. But right then, my standards had just gone up a notch or two. Oh, I knew he was scared to death. New kid in school? All of us staring at him? But he made his choice. Instead of being all meek and not making eye contact and just finding a desk, he stood there. Looked us all over and then looked away again, like he'd never seen a bigger collection of losers. I wonder if he'd been like that where he was before he came to Rockaway. I never thought about that before. You get to re-invent yourself when you move someplace new.

Second day, he sits down across from me in the cafeteria. He didn't have a lunch. Probably didn't have any money to buy one. I offered him my apple and some chips. He tells me he doesn't need my charity, but he grabs my chips anyway. I try to strike up a conversation, and he tells me I talk a lot.

"Nobody said you had to sit here," I say. He just laughs. Takes my apple and gets up and leaves.

I holler after him, "You think you're such a hotshot, but you're probably going to get your ass kicked."

He did, too. A couple of times. Bloody nose, eye swollen shut for almost a week. You don't just show up, a new kid, and act like that. People had to show him it's not his town.

Next day, I packed an extra sandwich.

Monologue from

The Sweet By and By

ALBERT
Elderly man

Are you here for me?

Oh, I know, there must be countless others in line ahead of me. But I have been ready for a long time.

If I've learned anything in my long, long life, it's that there are no guarantees. I think I've behaved myself for the most part, but there have been some lapses in there, that's for sure. Nothing that seemed likely to condemn me to the fiery pits, but, hey, I could be wrong.

People tell me, "Albert, you still have your health. You still have many good years left." They don't understand. There's more to it than that. *You* understand.

You know what I would do, if I could? I would give those good years to somebody else. Someone here, or perhaps to a young person with a serious illness. I would trade my good health for their poor health. Couldn't you talk to somebody about that? Find a way to redistribute those kinds of things?

It's all cockeyed. I'm used up. I'm ready. Yet, all around me, I see people who are desperately holding on. They're not done yet, for one reason or another. Somebody they're waiting to see one more time. Something left undone. Well, that's not me. I've done it all, everything I want to. Seen everyone I need to see. Said all I need to say.

I have lived a wonderful, wonderful life. Oh, it might not seem all that incredible to someone looking in at it. You, for instance. It probably seems like a fairly run-of-the-mill existence to somebody like you. I haven't jumped out of a plane. I haven't driven a race car. I was in the armed services, but the most action I saw was in a big room where I took things out of one file cabinet and put them in another. There have been some sorrows, of course, but who doesn't have those? A brother I lost at fifteen… A wife when she was barely fifty. I have no complaints. I believe I have done all the things I was set on this earth to do. I'm ready now for whatever is next. Good or bad, I'm just curious to see what it's going to be.

> ALBERT *faces forward, hands resting on his knees once more. Smiling, he closes his eyes, and heaves a contented sigh.*

Monologue from

Leaving Again

JAKE
A hitchhiker in his 20s

Lights up on single chair onstage. After a second, JAKE enters at a brisk trot. He mimes opening a car door and stepping inside, plopping himself down on the chair, slightly breathless.

Appreciate it. I've been standing out here a hell of a long time. Nobody's even slowed down until now. No one even makes eye contact. They just grip the wheel, act like they don't even see you, and whiz on by, you know?

People. They're assholes. Not *you*... necessarily. But most of them. ...I get it, you gotta be careful. Lot of creeps running around out there. But it's twenty degrees, for piss-sakes. All the self-respecting rapists and murderers are someplace where it's warm. It's just us harmless idiots and losers freezing our nuts off now.

(looking around as if gazing at the scenery)

This place hasn't changed a bit in twenty years. Still a stinking pile of shit in the middle of nowhere. Every tree, every building, every vacant lot looks just the same as it always has. Like I never left. Are you from around here? You've got my sympathies if you are, you sick bastard. *(beat)* No offense.

(sighs heavily)

You *can* go home again, no matter what they say. The question is, why do you want to?

(snort of bitter laughter)

I'm not one of those people who says stuff is always somebody else's fault. I've done my share of crap, I freely admit it. A lot of what's happened... well, I could have made some better choices, I know that. ... That was one of my caseworker's favorite phrases: *"Jake, you gotta learn to make better choices."*

No argument there. No argument, when you're twenty-five. ...Twenty. Or fifteen, even.

There was this guy in town. Back in the day. Maybe you'd remember him. Maybe you remember what happened. I dunno. Real nice fellow, that's what everybody said. Give you the shirt off his back. Do you a favor, any time of night or day. Everybody's friend...

His wife, now: Complete opposite. Quiet, kept to herself. A lot of people thought she was stuck-up. She didn't socialize much, wasn't real friendly. Drank a little. A little too much, some people said. Was always falling down, or running into things. Every time you'd see her, she was sporting some new injury. A bruise, a twisted ankle. A dislocated shoulder, one time. If you asked, she always said she was just naturally clumsy, and then she'd walk away. *"Well, maybe if she'd lay off the vodka, she'd be a little more coordinated,"* I heard a lady say one time.

One night, the cops got called to the house. The place looked like a war zone. Her husband, this real nice guy, is dead in the front hall, his head bashed in with a fireplace poker. The wife's got a black eye and some cracked ribs, and their kid—did I mention they had a kid?—has a bloody nose and a torn shirt. The wife and the kid say some intruders broke in and attacked them. But their stories don't quite add up, and the only fingerprints on the poker belong to the kid. It doesn't take a rocket scientist to figure out what really happened. Eventually, the kid gets sent to a correctional facility, and the wife goes on living in the house, still keeping to herself, still drinking a little too much. Except now, the funny thing is, she isn't so clumsy any more.

(he reflects on this for a few seconds, then smiles)

I don't even know why I brought it up. I guess it's just being back here after all this time. I just… I came to see somebody I haven't seen in a while. To say goodbye, I guess. They're not doing very well. I don't know how much longer she's gonna last, in fact. As I was leaving, she all of a sudden said, "Wait… I've got something to show you."

(he reaches into his shirt pocket to pull out a folded piece of heavy paper, which he proceeds to unfold and to study)

My birth certificate. Turns out, I was adopted. After all these years, I just now find this out. Can you believe this? Can you fucking believe it?

And the thing I don't get is… What, exactly, is she telling me? Am I supposed to be sad… or happy about this?

(he studies it for a moment, then refolds it and puts it back into his pocket. He looks at the unseen "driver" to his left)

I didn't even ask… Where you headed? No, that's all right, doesn't matter. As long as it's away from here.

(he faces forward once more. Lights fade)

END OF PLAY

Monologue from

Two Dates

CAROLYN
Early 20s to 40s

Thanks for dinner and the movie.

You don't need to walk me home. Why prolong this any longer than we already have? You don't want to be here. Not with me, anyway. In case you thought I wasn't picking up on your subtle hints.

I'm exhausted from trying to keep a conversation going, all the while pretending to ignore your thinly veiled hostility. This is not the date you wanted to be on tonight, am I right?

That's what I thought. So instead of just saying so, or, God forbid, just trying to fake a few pleasantries for one single evening, you do the passive-aggressive thing. You respond to anything I say with as few words as possible, you sigh and look away a lot, and you try to pick little fights, like about the movie I suggested we see. You've managed to be kind of rude, and kind of mean, but not exactly, so then it's really all my fault if I didn't have a good time, and you're in the clear.

Now I get to go home and wonder for the next three days just what it was about me that made you think I was barely worth the effort. Not pretty enough? Boobs not big enough? My ass too big? Not smart enough? Didn't gaze at you adoringly enough? And you know, the sad thing is… even though you're a jerk, I really will wonder all these things. I'll think, "What's so wrong with me that I can't even get a tool like that interested in me?"

So, congratulations. Despite everything, I still care what you think.

Good night.

Monologue from

Then Paupers Would Ride

KEITH
(18–30)

The more I tried to make her understand, the worse I made everything. All I wanted, I think, was for her to know that I was just a regular guy, not some crazy, not some sicko.

I just… in those few seconds… I watched it all fall apart. I just wanted to make her see that I was *normal.*

Even then, she was nice, she was trying to be nice. Trying to explain, trying so hard. And I could feel the distance between us get wider and wider, as she said that she'd never had "those kinds of feelings" about me. That we were friends, and that she was sorry if I'd misinterpreted things, or if she'd accidentally led me on in any way…

She smiled at me, and turned away. I didn't want her to go; I couldn't let it end that way.

I put my hand on her shoulder. "I just want to make you understand."

She yelled. Screamed, actually. I just… I wanted her to be quiet! I never meant… I was never going to…

"Please! Please, listen! I'm not going to hurt you!" …But… But… I did.

(fighting back emotion) I just wanted her to stop screaming...

I have no right to be sorry. ...But I am.

I used to think, "That's not who I am. I am not that person! I am not a person who does something like that." ...It was only later that I came to realize that I had it all backwards. I was never *not* that person. I just didn't know it until that night.

Monologue from

Close Enough to Admire

EUGENIA
(50s–80s)

After my surgery, I spent more than three months recuperating in that assisted-living facility and receiving physical therapy. I had two room-mates in that time, one with early senile dementia, another who was terminal but not far enough along to be in hospice care. I sat in the dining room and in the recreation hall with dozens of other residents. Some people were bright and alert, others angry and depressed, and still others never said a word at all. Some of us got to go home even-tually, and some knew they'd never leave. But do you know what the one common thread was that bound all of us, every last one? We were treated with condescension. Frequently well-intentioned, but still un-mistakably dismissive. Have you any idea, Ms. Clossen, how it feels when you are asking another person, someone who holds power and sway over you, for the simplest thing, and you see that patronizing smile cross their face, and you understand that they may or may not grant you your request, but in either event, they don't take you seri-ously? You're a child to them.

… Dignity. It's the loss of dignity I find more terrifying than anything.

I find it ironic that we come into this life, weak and helpless and entire-ly dependent on others to do even the most fundamental things for us. We get no say in what we wear, or when and what we eat, or where we go, or why. And if we live long enough, it all comes back to that again.

Am I using that term correctly? Irony? Maybe that's not what it is at all. Maybe...

... it just... is.

Monologue from

Six Sour Raspberries

LORI
(20–30)

So I'm going to say something different. You are lucky in one way. You will always get to remember him young and handsome and strong. Twenty, thirty, forty years from now, he will still be the same in your memory. I imagine you've had a whole lot of well-meaning people heaping a whole lot of moronic crap on you the past few days. And that's all this is, too. More moronic crap. So I understand if what you're thinking right now is, "I wish this bitch would just shut the hell up."

A long time ago, a friend of mine was in a car accident. I was very young, but I loved her very much. She was funny, and she was crazy, and in my parents' view, a bad influence on me. She suffered brain damage in the collision. I didn't get to see her for a long time afterward. And nothing anybody said could have prepared me…

Eventually, she came back to school. Her speech was permanently impaired, and one side of her face kind of sagged. She moved and reacted to everything slowly. She didn't seem like the girl I had known. Except when I looked into her eyes. There she was. I hated that. I hated her. It would have been easier if there had been no trace left. Instead, every day, I had to compare that person to the girl who'd been my friend. I felt robbed. That wasn't the way I wanted to remember her. And now, it's the only way I can. …Well, *there's* something about me I bet you didn't want to know.

Monologue from

Nocturne, Sort Of

ELLIOTT
(20s–up)

We all get hurt, you know. There's no one who hasn't had their heart stomped on at some point. We all arrive at love with a few bruises and scuff marks on us, that's just how it is. Nothing worthwhile comes easily.

But if you've got just one last date left in you, one more opportunity for the possibility of romance, take it. Lean out over that precipice. Make a spectacular dive. If you fail, fail with gusto. Be sure that the *splat!* you leave on the ground is visible for miles. That's what I intend to do. Years from now, people will walk by where it happened and point to it and say, "That—right there—is where Elliott Pulver crashed and burned. It was big, and it was ugly."

What does that prove? That I've removed all doubt. I may be bloodied and broken, but I know for sure. I won't be spending the rest of my days in a little room someplace, safe and intact, but still wondering.

What if those few seconds before I slammed into the ground were the best seconds of my life? And if it turns out they weren't, what does it matter? I'm toast, anyway. Metaphorically speaking.

Monologue from

A Room Where Life Won't Find You

DANA
(20s–up)

As soon as the elevator doors opened, it felt strange. Everything was exactly the same, like the hundred other times I've left the office. I was walking, listening to my heels clicking on the concrete. I thought, "This is just like in those movies where the woman is walking to her car and she hears footsteps, and at first, they're just her own... But then, there are other ones, and she starts walking faster..."

I read somewhere once that women, in particular, are more likely to be attacked if they act nervous and skittish. Just walk with a steady, confident gait, don't look around you furtively, don't act scared... But you want to be aware of your surroundings, don't you? You want to know if somebody is coming up behind you.

I didn't see anyone. I had my keys out. I got to my car, and was reaching for the handle. In the reflection of the window, there was this shadow, all of a sudden. Before I was even scared, I thought, "Where did he come from? Where was he hiding?" Then his hand was on the back of my neck. He shoved my face into the window, and I fell. I started to crawl under the car, but he grabbed me by the leg and pulled me back. He said, "If you make a noise, I'll twist your head around." That was his mistake, I think. It scared me so much that I started screaming. He was kicking me and trying to cover my mouth.

Then there was a car, thank God, coming from somewhere, and someone else yelling. Then the man was gone. I could hear him running. He hadn't been there, and then he was, and then he was gone again.

They found my bag on the sidewalk outside the building. Somebody brought it back. My driver's license was still in it. That's the only thing that has my address on it, thank heaven. The only thing. I didn't see his face. I never got to look at him.

I don't think I can go back to work. I don't think I can go back there. I'll never feel the same way there again.

Monologue from

Those Left to Face the Music

GABE
(Late 20s to late 30s)

Susan, as far as I'm concerned, he stopped being a member of this family a long time ago, back when he first did what he did. It's why I don't take your calls these days. It's why I change the subject or find a reason to leave when Mom brings it up. There's just so little to say about it. You want to welcome him back with open arms. I can understand it in Mom, maybe even forgive it a little bit—just a little—but not in you. You lived through the trial and the sentencing, and what it did to our family, same as me, and I can't sit with you and have a prolonged, thoughtful discussion about what we ought to do for Glenn.

I'm here today simply to tell you that, if he's grown an ounce of decency, which I seriously doubt, he will head straight for Mexico or parts unknown at least a thousand miles from here, and that will be the last any of us hear from him. But, since it's far more likely that he'll slink for home and for Mommy, so that she can take care of him, shield him from all those people saying mean things, and tell him how she knows he's just misunderstood, our only option is to let it happen and stand far away from the mud when it starts to fly.

And it will, Susan. Because what Mom is going to find out is that the same neighbors who shoveled her walks in winter and who brought casseroles after Dad died are capable of lobbing rocks through the windows or spray-painting hate messages on her car when they find out Glenn is living there again.

I've got my own family to worry about, Susan. If it was just her, I'd do anything. Move her in with Gina and me. Help her buy a new place. But she's making a choice. One that I can't support.

Monologue from

Remaining in Orbit

LISSIE
(Late teens–up)

I think you're afraid to ask why he gave me a key, regardless of the answer. It might mean that he equates me with you. You, coming here, working for him, seeing to his little needs all those years. And me. Some… truck stop waitress upstart. And still, he gave me a key. Doesn't that just fill you with righteous indignation? Or worse yet… What if he gave me a key because I mean something different to him than you do? You tell me, Ginnie. Which of those things bothers you the most?

It's okay… to want something from him. It's perfectly natural. There's nothing wrong with telling him. Because if you're waiting for him to notice, well, you could be waiting a long time. I think you already have been. Just remaining in someone's orbit isn't enough. Not when it's someone like Hen, who doesn't notice, or who chooses not to notice most everything around him, not unless it's written down in black and white.

Don't count on the fact that someday he's going to look up from his pages… and pages and pages… of crap, and suddenly see you in a brand-new light. Maybe he will. Or maybe he'll look up and look right past you at somebody else.

It would just be so sad, is all I'm saying. If you were hoping for something more. And you never told him.

Monologue from

Remaining in Orbit

GINNIE
(40s–up)

I don't hate her.

I hate you. I hate you, and I hate myself. For all the days and months that I'll never have back. I think I would like to hate her, too, but what's the point, really? If anything, I should be grateful. I'm free to get on with my life now. Whatever that may be. Maybe, someday, when I'm feeling more charitable, I'll write her a thank-you note.

There was an afternoon, maybe six weeks ago, when I was working and you were out. She showed up here. I hadn't seen her in a few weeks, and you hadn't mentioned her, so I thought maybe we'd seen the last of her. But no. She said… she said the most audacious thing. And I started thinking, and in one awful moment, I knew she was right. About everything. About me. About you. She said I should say something to you, tell you…

I couldn't. Because, all of a sudden, I knew how you felt. She seemed to think it was a race, and whoever talked to you first would win. But I understood that it was already over. No contest.

Monologue from

Someone Else's Life

ALAN
(50s–up)

When my older daughter Jeanine was fifteen, she ran away from home. It was two weeks before the police found her. Rose and I were frantic. But here's the thing I've never told my wife, not to this very day. *(pause)* I knew she was going to do it. I think maybe I knew even before Jeanine herself did. She was the sweetest kid until she hit puberty and then, overnight, she became the devil's child. She made life hell for everyone—us, her brothers, her sister. One Sunday, the family was out to brunch. Jeanine was studying the menu. Our eyes just happened to meet as she looked up, and that's when I knew. I couldn't begin to tell you how. We just looked at each other for half a second. She smiled, and I smiled, and in that fleeting instant, I knew. I thought, "Oh, God, she's going to do something crazy."

A few days later, she was gone. Vanished. I tried to tell myself it was something she needed to do. Whether it was to see what life was like away from her family, or if it was a way to hurt her mother and me. That thought kept me going through the first week. Then I started to crumble. Rose had become a zombie, shuffling through the house, eyes red and puffy. All the scenarios I'd been able to keep at bay came crashing in. Jeanine had been kidnapped. Raped. Was dead somewhere, or dying. And I could have stopped it, if I'd just done something.

When the cops brought her home, she walked in, looked us over, and said to her little sister, "If you got into any of my stuff, I'll kick your ass." …I have never wanted to backhand someone across the face as much as I did my daughter in that moment.

So, if you really have any interest in how I'm feeling, I'm marveling at how fast a person's feelings can change from one second to the next. From absolute relief and joy to white, blind rage. Not all that interesting, is it?

Monologue from

The Last Word

MAGGIE
(20s–40s)

Are you happy? …Has this really turned out to be what you wanted?

Okay. Well, then… good. I guess I can't begrudge you that, at least. Everyone deserves to be happy.

I was furious at the time, though. I had some dark thoughts. Murderous ones. I wanted to kill you. …No, *really.* I looked into buying a gun. But you know I hate loud noises. So I hired a guy to do it for me.

I told him it could be his choice. It didn't have to be a bullet. He could run over you with a car, if that was easier. Or push you out a window or off a balcony. Stab you on a busy street, in the middle of a crowd. *(shrugging offhandedly)* Murderous thoughts.

After a while, I realized you couldn't help it. People don't always get to pick who they fall in love with. And when I stopped to consider that, most of my anger—the fury—started to go away. You wanted to be intimate with a man instead of with me. That wasn't my fault. There wasn't anything that I could have done differently. Except maybe grow a penis.

Oh, well. It's a new day.

About the Author

Colorado native Scott Gibson is an award-winning playwright and the author of six novels. Gibson's plays have been performed from New York to Los Angeles and filmed for television. He particularly focuses on lifelike characters and plots that touch on the humorous and dramatic. Gibson earned a BA in English from the University of Northern Colorado and has worked as a technical editor and blogger. When he's not working on his next novel, he volunteers with animal shelters and enjoys Colorado's beautiful outdoors by jogging, hiking and cycling.